How Green is Your Smartphone?

Digital Futures Series

How Green is Your Smartphone?

RICHARD MAXWELL AND
TOBY MILLER

polity

First published in 2020 by Polity Press

Polity Press
65 Bridge Street
Cambridge CB2 1UR, UK

Polity Press
101 Station Landing
Suite 300
Medford, MA 02155, USA

ISBN-13: 978-1-5095-3471-5 (hardback)
ISBN-13: 978-1-5095-3472-2 (paperback)

A catalogue record for this book is available from the British Library.

Typeset in 11 on 15 Adobe Garamond by
Servis Filmsetting Ltd, Stockport, Cheshire
Printed and bound in Great Britain by TJ International Limited

The publisher has used its best endeavours to ensure that the URLs for external websites referred to in this book are correct and active at the time of going to press. However, the publisher has no responsibility for the websites and can make no guarantee that a site will remain live or that the content is or will remain appropriate.

Every effort has been made to trace all copyright holders, but if any have been overlooked the publisher will be pleased to include any necessary credits in any subsequent reprint or edition.

For further information on Polity, visit our website: politybooks.com

CONTENTS

The Economist identified 2019 as "peak smartphone." The "most successful consumer product in history" had reached four billion of the world's five and half billion adults. Over 95 percent of Americans owned a cellphone, and smartphones comprised 77 percent of that total. The highest concentration was among educated 19 to 49-year-old city dwellers (Pew Research Center, 2018). South Korea topped the world's list with 94 percent smartphone ownership, and the trend was similar throughout developed economies, with Japan, Germany, Italy, France, and the UK slowly catching up to US levels (Poushter, Bishop, and Chwe, 2018).

Cultural, social, economic, health, and ecological corollaries of peak smartphone have accompanied this expansion. Umberto Eco reimagines David Lean's *Dr Zhivago* (1965) for our own times, recalling: "the tragedy of Zhivago, who after years sees Lara from the tram (remember the final scene of the film?), doesn't manage to get off in time, and dies. Had they both had a mobile phone, would we have had a happy ending?"

(2014, p. viii). The smartphone is a reassuring talisman: we may find ourselves one day on unfamiliar terrain, but can find our way out through its mapping functions. We may wander into a "dodgy" part of town, but can rely on it to communicate our whereabouts to loved ones or the state apparatus (Morley, 2017).

Meanwhile, the companies concerned revel in cell-phone saturation of the world's ears, eyes, and fingers. Apple says "We believe everyone should be able to do what they love with iPhone."[1] Samsung invites customers to "meet our latest and greatest innovation" – its Galaxy S10.[2] Google boasts that the Pixel 3 is "Everything you wish your phone could do."[3] That all sounds rather grand – stylish new phones that give us what we want. Trust Apple, trust Samsung, trust Google. But a 2019 report on the Mobile World Congress announced in a letter to "Dear Visionaries" that the industry was "suffering from a combination of split personality disorder and ADHD" (ABI Research for Visionaries/MWC 19 Barcelona, 2019). That diagnosis derived from the differing interests of two fractions of capital – phone manufacturers versus carriers. And there was no room

[1] https://www.apple.com/iphone-xr/only-iphone/
[2] https://www.samsung.com/us/mobile/galaxy-s10/
[3] https://store.google.com/us/product/pixel_3?hl=en-US

"The most successful consumer product in history…"

in this world of visionaries for either party to consider whether their phones were green.

Because the diffusion of these devices has been more rapid than their innovation, sales finally began to diminish in 2018: there is a dwindling number of first-time customers left to corral. But even though improvements have become ever more marginal, the industry can count on 2.8 billion people replacing their phones every two years ("The Maturing," 2019). Meanwhile, the consumer market is slowly becoming less significant than demand from military, medical, meat, and manufacturing segments of the economy (ABI Research for Visionaries/MWC 19 Barcelona, 2019).

For all that, digital utopians continue to fete the phone's popularity, reach, and effects. According to Bell Labs, "more than 5 zettabytes of data … pass through the network every year. That is the equivalent of everyone in the world tweeting non-stop for more than 100 years."[4] For Edgar Morin, the instantaneity of phone communication means that our "world is made more and more whole" (1999). In similar vein, Ulrich Beck says the cellphone has altered "sociological categories of time, space, place, proximity and distance" as it "makes those who are absent present, always and

---

[4] http://www.alcatel-lucent.com/bell-labs/GWATT

everywhere" (2002: 31). It is said that one day the smartphone may even provide material clues to the way we lived:

> The phone has much in common with the portable artifacts of a more traditional archaeology, like flint hand-axes or pottery vessels … an object scaled to fit the human world … shaped to fit the hand and fingers, and has action capabilities … orientated towards other parts of the body … (Edgeworth 2010: 143)

But there's another side to this seeming cornucopia. The World Privacy Forum proposes that we inhabit a *One-Way Mirror Society*, where power accretes to corporations through the supposedly even-handed tool of interactivity (Dixon, 2010). Former true-believers at *Wired* magazine see the internet undone by the corporatization of knowledge and the sealed-set model of phone applications (Anderson and Wolff, 2010). Dan Schiller describes the displacement and deracination of modern life as a blend of individuation with mobility. He argues that political-economic arrangements mean that mobile telephony has emerged in a form befitting divided societies (2007).

And, while the gap in mobile-phone ownership

between rich and poor has narrowed in the US, nearly 30 percent of adults with household incomes below $30,000 don't own a smartphone, and over 40 percent of such households lack broadband, a desktop, or a laptop. About 26 percent of low-income Americans with smartphones but no home broadband depend on cellular services for network connectivity. That number has doubled since 2013 (Anderson and Kumar, 2019).

Globally, the smartphone gap between rich and poor regions is shrinking, though inequalities in access and service standards remain (Silver and Johnson, 2018). The International Telecommunications Union (ITU) reports that "[a]lmost the whole world population now lives within range of a mobile-cellular network signal," and more than half are online (2018a, p. 2). The ITU notes (and promotes) the growing importance of mobile cellular telecommunications for economic growth in Africa, the Arab States, Asia, and Latin America (2018a, p. 4).

But by its own reckoning, there is immense variation within the Global South in smartphone ownership, access to mobile networks, and, perhaps most importantly, affordable, fast, and reliable connections (2018a, pp. 104–6 and 125–30; Alvarez, 2014; Bianchi, 2015). In addition, much of the Global South has a very significant gender gap in access to smartphones (Bhandari, 2019).

Ignoring these obdurate limitations, the ITU, the telecommunications industry, and electronics manufacturers insist that mobile cellular communication will inevitably and beneficially expand from the wealthy countries where they are headquartered. The industry's hype has an imperious ring: we are heading inexorably toward the next stage of technological and human progress and pleasure. Mobile communication will be foundational.

In the face of such breathless predictions, we should keep in mind that the idea of technological progress has only been around since the nineteenth century, when it was deployed as propaganda "to deny the legitimacy and rationality" of organized opposition to industrial machinery (Noble, 1995). The Luddites, famous for sometimes destroying machines they feared would ruin their livelihoods and the quality of their craft, "did not believe in technological progress, nor could they have; the alien idea was invented after them, to try to prevent their recurrence" (Noble, 1995, p. 2).

They weren't opposed to new technology *per se*, only to boosters' obliviousness to its undemocratic designs and socially destructive deployment. We adhere to that critique in our examination of the smartphone as an emblem of technological progress. The world has been subject to the incessant promotion of smartphone innovations for over a decade. Such rhetoric ignores the central topics of this book: environmental harm, labor exploitation, and the connivance of industry with anti-science propaganda.

It's ironic that *The Economist* used an adjective generally applied to the "terror" of running out of petroleum – "peak oil" – to describe super-saturation of the world cellphone market. For both industries have played malevolent roles in our planetary crisis. And both relate to the concept "green" in our title. "Green" can signify displeasure, even disgust. For example, "he turned green" or "it's indefensible to have green lawns in LA." But the meaning of the term is more complex than that. It is simultaneously serene, beneficial, disturbing, corrupted, radical, and conservative: green consumption, green certification, new (green) deal, and greenwashing.

In the late 1960s and early 1970s, the word "pollution" was in vogue to explain environmental hazards. Both a ubiquitous and a local sign, it seemed to be everywhere, yet isolable. The problems it described occurred when particular waterways, neighborhoods, or fields suffered negative externalities from mining, farming, and manufacturing. The issue was how to restore these places to their prior state: pristine, unspoiled, enduring. Pollution was about corporate malfeasance, governmental neglect, and public ignorance, and how to remedy their malign impact. It could be cleaned up if governments compelled companies to do so – and would soon be over, once those involved understood the problem.

But when greenhouse gases, environmental racism, global warming, occupational health, and environmental imperialism appeared on the agenda, pollution reached beyond national boundaries and became ontological, threatening the very Earth that gives and sustains life, and doing so in demographically unequal ways.

A word was found to describe the values and forms of life that encompassed a planetary consciousness to counter this disaster, as per the utopias of world government that had animated transnational imaginations for decades: "green" emerged to displace the more negative and limited term "pollution," signifying both new possibilities and a greater and more global sense of urgency. Its purview expanded from waterways and work places to populations and the planet.

This beguilingly simple syntagm, "green," was quickly transformed into a complex polysemic *mélange*. Today, it can refer to local, devolved, non-corporate empowerment, or international consciousness and institutional action. The term is invoked by both conservatives, who emphasize maintaining the world for future generations, and radicals, who stress anti-capitalist, post-colonial, feminist perspectives. "Green" may highlight the disadvantages of technology, as a primary cause of environmental difficulties, or hail such innovations as future saviors, via devices and processes yet to be invented that will alleviate global warming. It can favor state and international regulation, or be skeptical of public policy. It may encourage individual consumer responsibility, or question localism by contrast with collective action. It can reflect left–right axes of politics, or argue that they should be transcended, because neither statism nor individualism can fix the dangers we confront.

This massive, conflictual expansion in meaning has generated a wide array of instrumental uses. So, green environments are promoted as exercise incentives (Gladwell et al., 2013), encouragements for consumers to use quick-response codes (Atkinson, 2013), ways of studying whether plants communicate through music (Gagliano, 2012), attempts to push criminology toward interrogating planetary harm (Lynch et al., 2013), gimmicks for recruiting desirable employees (Renwick et al., 2012), and techniques for increasing labor productivity (Woo et al., 2013).

In accord with this expansion, Green political parties now address labor conditions, immigration policies, human rights, industrial growth, and climate science (Miller, 2015). That does not mean the origins of the term are lost – simply that the material state of play has required this semantic expansion due to an accretion of meaning over time and space, as the state of our crisis becomes clearer, both to science and to activism. In short, "green" has come to stand for the good life – not merely our own, but that of our fellow animals and our collective descendants yet to be born. It stands for a new solidarity that takes off from climate science to seek a better, more secure future that transcends the usual homilies and shibboleths of individual agency or investor returns.

Climate science leaves little doubt that humans have made the Earth an inhospitable place for life to flourish. The latest, and most urgent, report from the United Nations Intergovernmental Panel on Climate Change warns that we have about twelve years to make radical changes to our carbon-emitting ways, or disaster awaits (Watts, 2018). The US National Climate Assessment, a project of thirteen Federal departments and agencies, reports that the country faces imminent risks from rising sea levels, wildfires, drought, floods, atmospheric warming, and a weakening of its ecosystems' ability to absorb carbon emissions and other greenhouse gases (US Global Change Research Program, 2018). Ninety-seven percent of scientists say humans are responsible for global warming and must radically change our behavior to save the planet's biosphere, ecosystems, and inhabitants. There is a disturbing gap between these urgent warnings from climate scientists and public awareness of the ecological crisis. Equally alarming is the fact that recent surveys show the US population believes only 49 percent of scientists subscribe to the reality of climate change, with over a quarter erroneously discerning "a lot of disagreement" among them (Marlon et al., 2018).

Public uncertainty is a powerful inhibitor of political action and contributes to acceptance of atmospheric warming. But there is hope. Americans are increasingly concerned by global warming, even if most do not understand its causes. Perhaps this anxiety is inevitable as we experience increasingly extreme weather systems, destructive "natural" events, and ecosystem losses associated with climate change (Schwartz, 2019).

There is also a spirited and growing green youth movement around the world protesting political inaction over the eco-crisis. Young activists are standing up to billionaires and Jurassic politicians, telling them to their faces to cut the bullshit and act on the science (Wearden and Carrington, 2019). A generation born in an era of peak disaster from global warming will not tolerate the craven politics of world leaders beholden to barons of industry and finance, fossil-fuel giants, and technology moguls. Tens of thousands of Western

"We have about twelve years to make radical changes to our carbon-emitting ways, or disaster awaits."

European school pupils went on strike in the winter of 2019 with the slogans #FridaysForFuture and "There's no Planet B" ("Children's Climate," 2019). Hence also women deciding to #BirthStrike because they feel unable to guarantee climate security to future generations (Doherty, 2019), and the efforts of Extinction Rebellion.[5] Their task is huge – UN Secretary-General Antonio Guterres warns that the political will to combat climate change is "fading" (quoted in "Political Will," 2019). Public support for action to stem our eco-crisis remains a work in progress, building slowly as people come to grasp the urgency of a planetary problem. But there are signs of a new citizenry ready to act on their environmental commitments. *Nature* and the *British Medical Journal* alike drew inspiration from #FridaysForFuture (Fisher, 2019; Stott et al., 2019).

The Book You Hold in Your Hands

How Green Is Your Smartphone? is informed by the logic and research of climate and environmental science and political-economic and ethnographic social science, the ethical and political commitments of environmental

[5] https://rebellion.earth

movements, and young activists' zero tolerance for the status quo as they seek new economic arrangements and green environments for work, rest, and play.

We've been teaching about these issues in several countries for over a decade, and have not always found it easy to narrow the gap between scientific and public knowledge, especially when questioning cellphones. They have become part of people's very senses of self. Hence a polemical volume that takes a side in this elemental struggle, at the same time as it strives to communicate the current state of academic agreement and disagreement, alongside the work of governments, activists, and the media.

Of course, many people don't think about the fate of the Earth. We didn't write this book for them. They might pick it up just the same: like most people, they own a cellphone. Those who do so will discover that a crucial, pocket-sized part of their electronic lives is connected to a whole world in need of help. For we hope that this wee polemic will show that even the smallest changes to how we think about our digital world can contribute to a new understanding of the good life – one that prioritizes the biosphere, ecology, and a balance between human existence and the Earth's life-support systems.

We remain some distance from that goal. In the

early twenty-first century, the good life continues to be defined by material growth based on consumerism. The smartphone stands out in that seductive *laissez-faire* fable as a symbol of progress and plenitude. By contrast, this book examines the material reality and social impact of these digital technologies, with a particular focus on environmental risks linked to cellphones and similar devices.

We're not interested in shaming users, or returning society to a time prior to mobile communication. We want to explain the environmental risks associated with these devices in a social context, and how they can be reduced. Our aim is to delineate a role for the smartphone in a greener communications system. Understanding the material characteristics of smartphones helps us identify guidelines to make them greener, on personal and planetary scales alike.

The chapters that follow urge readers to:

- *Outsmart your smartphone*
- *Acknowledge that the greenest smartphone is the one you already own*; and
- *Call bullshit on anti-science propaganda*

Outsmart Your Smartphone

Mobile cellular communication relies on network connections. Radiofrequency radiation bounces back and forth from our phones to cell towers and wireless transmitters. Exposure to this radiation has been linked to potential health risks, including cancer. We can reduce such possibilities, even without clear guidance from the industry or its regulators.

The Federal Communications Commission (FCC), which certifies cellphone safety in the US, says "no scientific evidence currently establishes a definite link between wireless device use and cancer or other illnesses" (Federal Communications Commission, 2018). If this is true, why does it issue guidelines that limit public exposure to radiofrequency radiation? Cellular telephones must not surpass radiation levels of 1.6 watts per kilogram (W/kg), which is an average of energy absorbed by one gram of tissue according to the US testing standard (Federal Communications Commission, n.d.). This is known as the Specific Absorption Rate (SAR).

Be aware that the manufacturers themselves decide the safe distance between phone and human tissue to meet SAR guidelines; the government does not handle this for us. Apple says you're safe in exceeding 1.6 W/kg of exposure if you hold a phone five centimeters from your head; Samsung says fifteen centimeters is safe; other manufacturers recommend ten centimeters. It's up to them. That's a problem for cellphone users, and another good reason we need to outsmart our phones.

SAR levels matter. Most people hold phones against their heads and bodies. Studies of exposure to radio-frequency radiation at zero distance show SAR levels twice as high as the regulatory limit, and in some tests, three to four times higher. In 2017, France's Agence nationale des fréquences (ANFR) [National Frequency Agency] found that most "phones exceed government radiation limits when tested the way they are used, next to the body" (Environmental Health Trust, 2018b). The ANFR's study has been likened to "dieselgate," the revelation that Volkswagen lied for years about emissions from its diesel-engine cars, which the company had rigged to emit atypically low levels in controlled conditions. "Phonegate," as some have called it, sheds a critical light on the mendacity of the telecommunications industry.

If SAR is so important a guideline for the safe use of a cellphone, why don't most of us know about it?

You might be surprised to learn that your phone includes instructions about SAR levels; you just haven't been told where to find them. In the US, the FCC requires phone manufacturers to inform consumers if their products meet regulatory guidelines for exposure levels. They comply, but in a sneaky way. Most phones have a legal notice about "RF exposure" buried in their settings. It takes five steps to find them on a typical iPhone, or you can review them on Apple's website.[6] Other manufacturers make it equally hard, or more difficult, to locate instructions for safe use; it's as if they designed a feature to make smartphones stupid about this topic. Compare that to health warnings on cigarette packets, with their alarming words and graphic images.

A study conducted for the Canadian Broadcasting Corporation found that 81 percent of Canadians did not know their government's guidelines on cellphone use, or that phones themselves explained how to lessen radiation exposure (Mission Research, 2017; *The Secret*, 2017). We assume the lack of public knowledge elsewhere is similar. If the industry is required to tell us about possible health risks, but effectively conceals that information, we must ask: What else is it hiding? One way to answer that question is to review legislation around the world that compels phone manufacturers to put explicit health warnings on their packaging. France and Israel have passed such laws. But where other

---

[6] https://www.apple.com/legal/rfexposure/

countries have tried, the telecommunications industry has lobbied to oppose explicit labelling. In the US and Canada, bills were proposed, then shot down under pressure from industry groups (Environmental Health Trust, 2018a).

That leads us to a third point about personal health. A chorus of concerns has arisen around cellphone addiction. These have largely centered on children and families, with corresponding remedies that are highly individual. We review those anxieties, as well as public concerns that smartphone distraction has become a key factor in traffic injuries and deaths. Finally, we examine the possible diseases caused by exposure to radiation.

For now, it's important to stress that many scientific studies suggest there may be a causal link between cellphone radiofrequency radiation and a number of illnesses, including cancer. The results are not definitive. But based on the scientific knowledge we have examined, precaution is prescribed. Please be careful not to store or use your phone next to your body. Rely on wired ear phones, text, or speaker phones when possible. Outsmart your smartphone.

In general, we hope that an abiding legacy of green politics and theory will be the development and installation of the precautionary principle into everyday life and policymaking.[7] That principle is opposed to conventional cost–benefit analysis, which looks at the pluses and minuses of consumer satisfaction versus safety. Instead, it places the burden of proof onto proponents of industrial processes to show they are environmentally safe, the idea being to avoid harm rather than deal with risks once they are already in motion: prevention, not cure.

The Greenest Smartphone is the One You Already Own

Retaining the smartphone you already own is your greenest option. First, we point to hazards faced by extractive and factory workers who make these devices for us. Their workplace pressures intensify each time consumers order the latest model smartphone. By keeping smartphones for as long as possible, users can de-pressurize the labor process.

Second, we look at smartphones among an array of digital screen technologies that use sizeable amounts of energy and natural resources, both in their production,

---

[7] https://www.sehn.org/precautionary-principle-understanding-sci
ence-in-regulation

through the emission of greenhouse gases and hazardous pollutants, and in their useful lifetimes, because of their need for what is often coal-fired power to recharge and connect to network systems and data services.

If we combine emissions from manufacturing and the electricity that powers network and data-storage facilities, smartphones and other so-called terminal platforms produce about 1.4 percent of the world's total carbon footprint. Most of that happens during manufacturing; over the useful lifetime of a phone, relatively few greenhouse-gas emissions are produced (Malmodin and Lundén, 2018, pp. 28–9). Extending that life by keeping them longer makes them greener.

Otherwise, they become poisonous waste. According to the United Nations University (UNU), "Electronic waste, or e-waste, refers to all items of electrical and electronic equipment and its parts that have been discarded by its owner as waste without the intent of re-use."[8] When we throw smartphones away or "recycle" them, they frequently end up as toxic e-waste, the fastest-growing element in global waste streams: about 46 to 50 million metric tons, and growing by three to four percent annually. Cellphones alone comprise approximately ten percent of those figures (Baldé et al., 2018,

---

[8] http://www.step-initiative.org/

pp. 39–40). The average period people in the global North keep their phones is less than two years. This is out of habit, not loss of functionality. Retaining them for as long as possible can lighten the flow of e-waste to an already overburdened system.

Calling Bullshit on Anti-Science Propaganda

Like the tobacco and fossil-fuel industries, telecommunications firms have no compunction about using public relations to "war-game science" via campaigns that spread doubt and confusion about ecological problems, from climate change to radiofrequency radiation. The trick involves discrediting researchers who report evidence of harm, while backing scholarship that reports reassuring findings. That scam worked for tobacco corporations for decades, with disastrous results for public health.

But by the time we get to Chapter 3, we'll be smarter than our phones. We'll have figured out how to make them greener, and be ready to take on industry scoundrels and gullible journalists. With the air cleared of polluting propaganda, our brief conclusion can offer ideas about what should happen next.

We take these matters very seriously, not only because

we are concerned consumers of this technology, but because we have been unknowing stakeholders in its development. Click wheels, multi-touch screens, global-positioning systems, lithium-ion batteries, signal compression, hyper-text markup language, liquid-crystal displays, and a number of other innovations were the result of government funding from publicly funded entities such as the US Defense Advanced Research Projects Agency, the European Organization for Nuclear Research, the US Department of Energy, the CIA, the National Science Foundation, the US Navy, the US Army Research Office, the National Institutes of Health, the US Department of Defense – and research universities (Mazzucato, 2015). We paid taxes that made smartphones and their immediate predecessors possible – that's right, taxes – and private corporations profited.

So, it's important to acknowledge that we have a responsibility to encourage smartphone owners such as ourselves to go beyond an appreciation of these devices' utility and understand our relation to the harm they cause. As well as holding onto our phones for as long as possible, we should endeavor to keep up with the related knowledge on technology's medical, cultural, social, and environmental impact, from media effects to corporate swindles.

We researched and wrote much of this book on

mobile devices – that's the paradox of a project that aims to make smartphones greener from within as well as beyond the boundaries of their guileful promises. Our hope is that *How Green Is Your Smartphone?* will enable readers who don't have the time to delve into the relevant studies to contribute to public debate about these gadgets. It's urgently needed.

ONE

Outsmart Your Smartphone

Set your smartphone to Airplane Mode and find a spot without WiFi transmitters nearby. If possible, read under natural light. We'll explain why these precautions can outsmart your cellphone.

The Allure

Our love for smartphones is more durable than the phones themselves. They are fragile, so we encase them in protective plastic. Their batteries fade just when we need them. And as they age, they stop learning and growing – their younger siblings are deemed more knowledgeable and powerful. Everything about them should question our faith. Yet we remain true believers that cellphones' DNA is wonderful, and new generations necessarily bring major improvements. We have embraced wireless mobile technology so fully that many of us feel adrift without it. By some estimates, Americans touch their cellphones 2,617 times a day

"We have embraced wireless mobile technology so fully that many of us feel adrift without it."

(Naftulin, 2016). Twenty-six percent of all users are constantly online, and 39 percent of 18 to 29 year-olds (Perrin and Jiang, 2018). We depend on cellphones for dates, phone numbers, and meeting times. We assign mental chores to them and trust they'll remember what we cannot (Wegner and Ward, 2013). Users even focus on "Battling a Monster of a Location-Based Augmented-Reality Game While Descending Stairs" (Ma et al., 2019), so touching is their faith that phones will protect them while enabling stupid conduct.

Social scientists have mixed feelings about the social impact of smartphones. On the one hand, they can broaden channels of communication, enhance personal safety, integrate family life, strengthen peer groups, facilitate rendezvous, and allow users to produce content, create their own languages, and add special features like customized cases and ring tones – all of which makes us feel unique and important (Castells et al., 2007). *Bourgeois* economists see these benefits spreading worldwide, with effects that allegedly include energized markets in the Global South, "the complete elimination of waste," and massive reductions in poverty and corruption (Jensen, 2007).

This utopian alchemy of truth and beauty endows mobile telephony with magical powers that allow users to transcend geography, sovereignty, and poverty (Ogan et al., 2009). This magic is said to make consumers into producers, free the disabled from confinement, encourage new subjectivities, reward intellect and competitiveness, link people across cultures, and allow billions of flowers to bloom. In a post-political cornucopia, consumption is privileged while labor and the environment are forgotten.

On the flip side, phones may deepen rather than diminish social fragmentation and cause a novel form of inequality, because without them, you lack access to the new sociality of the twenty-first century – constant connection (Castells et al., 2007). Some studies suggest that the frenzy to stay connected negatively affects relations between friends and lovers, increasing insecurity and dissatisfaction (Lapierre and Lewis, 2018) and diminishing interest in sex (Chang, 2016). We might love cellphones more than we love each other.

It's significant that the world's leading media ratings company, Nielsen, celebrated the fact that: "Africa is in the midst of a technological revolution, and nothing illustrates that fact [more] than the proliferation of mobile phones." Then it casually noted that "more Africans have access to mobile phones than to clean drinking water" (Hutton, 2011). This vision of technological progress cannot conceal the environmental racism (or environmental neo-colonialism) at its roots.

When roughly half the population of Africa lacks potable water, the celebration of mobile communication at the expense of public health is appalling.[1]

As we discuss below, this bias runs deep in the telecommunications industry. It characterizes the imperious industry hype noted in our Introduction. Challenging such attitudes is central to outsmarting our smartphones.

Are We Addicted?

How often have we left home patting our pockets or rifling through our purses to confirm we have our phones? It's not unusual for people to say they feel naked without their smartphones: they have digitally disappeared (McSpadden, 2019). No searches, no maps, no social media – no them. Forty-six percent of Americans in 2017 avowed they could not survive without their cellphones (Beren, 2018). Forty percent of US consumers worry that they overuse phones (60 percent of people

---

[1] In 2014, there were 629 million mobile-phone subscriptions in Africa and 742 million people had access to potable water, out of a population of well over a billion (http://mobiforge.com/research-analysis/global-mobile-statistics-2014-part-a-mobile-subscribers-handset-market-share-mobile-operators#subscribers)

aged between 18 and 34), while 63 percent seek to cut down phone time (Deloitte, 2018). Many suffer from "phantom vibration syndrome," wrongly believing they can feel their phones vibrating with messages (Drouin et al., 2012). Fear of being disconnected has been linked to the regret, depression, and anxiety that accompany the loss of putative internet pleasures, from gaming, gossiping, and gambling to pornography, photography, and philandery. Such effects signify internet businesses' successful use of algorithmic addiction, much as nicotine addiction works for the tobacco industry.

Smartphones have also created a new nightmare for public-health professionals, because sex workers at risk of sexually transmitted diseases increasingly communicate with clients by phone and travel to a widening variety of places to ply their trade. This makes them less easy to advise and assist than when they work at known material sites. Illegal gambling is also facilitated, putting chronic users at risk (Mahapatra et al., 2012; Agur, 2015).

In addition to such woes, new opportunities of course present themselves. Stanford University's Persuasive Technology Lab promises students "insight into how computing products … can be designed to change what people believe and what they do."[2] The program

[2] https://captology.stanford.edu/

instructs individuals to manipulate others (and avoid being manipulated) through "captology" – the study of how humans get trapped in technology through algorithms like those that make slot machines addictive (Fogg, 2003; Rushkoff, 2016, p. 91; Rushkoff, 2019, pp. 65–7).

Nomophobia – short for "no mobile phobia" – has been invented to characterize our mental dependence on these things. A concept coined by the UK Post Office, it is now part of widespread investigations into the isolation and even fear induced by being without a cellphone – to the point where there is agitation for nomophobia to be a formal diagnostic instrument of mental illnesses (Yildirim and Correia, 2015; Bragazzi and Del Puente, 2014; Valdesolo, 2015). Hence also the development of a psychological "Young Adult Attachment to Phone Scale," complete with the wonderful acronym, "YAPS" (Trub and Barbot, 2016) and an "Internet Addiction Scale" (Kwon et al., 2013). Neuroscientists merrily refer to "Smartphone Addiction" as the "Psychopathology of Everyday Life in the 21st Century" (Lin et al., 2017). Mobile addiction has sparked the greatest public curiosity in wealthy countries and among affluent consumers in the Global South (Howard, 2017). The malady is often associated with US-style hyper-consumerism (Prideaux, 2015).[3] The unique quality of electronic technology to stimulate addictive behavior can also be traced to ideas of progress associated with the "technological sublime," the quasi-sacred power that industrial societies have bestowed upon modern high-tech machinery and feats of engineering, whose awesome, hypnotic, and scary qualities are said to draw us inescapably toward them, once they are beautified by seductive design and marketing (Nye, 1994 and 2006).

Hence the noted media theorist Paul Virilio's lament:

[I]t is now necessary to impose silence in restaurants and places of worship or concert halls. One day, following the example of the campaign to combat nicotine addiction, it may well be necessary to put up signs of the "Silence Hospital" variety at the entrance to museums and exhibition halls to get all those "communication machines" to shut up and

---

³ The idea of internet addiction is the latest in a long litany of ailments associated with modern life – in the nineteenth century, the medical doctor named George Beard said Americans suffered from "neurasthenia" caused by the accelerating rhythms of rail, telegraph, and the daily press. William James nicknamed this new pathology Americanitis. Theodore Roosevelt and Jane Addams were among its victims, and new potions of suspect origin were marketed to soothe the suffering. Freud agreed that such neuroses of civilization multiplied with growing affluence, but countered that they were due in large part to faulty unconscious processes rather than external stimuli (Osnos, 2011).

put an end to the all too numerous cultural exercises in SOUND and LIGHT. (2004: 76)

The spreading belief that internet addiction more generally is a malady has inspired new forms of treatment (Aguayo, 2015). In 2018, the World Health Organization (WHO) identified an internet gaming disorder and Britain's National Health Service created a Centre for Internet Disorders (Marsh, 2018). Many pioneers of our wireless world worry about their children's exposure to glowing screens. Tim Cook banned his nephew from social media, Bill and Melinda Gates made cellphones off-limits to their pre-teens, and Steve Jobs wouldn't let his children near an iPad. John Lilly, former head of Mozilla, explained to his teenage son that "somebody wrote code to make you feel this way." Chris Anderson, editor of *Wired* magazine, calls screen addiction "closer to crack cocaine" than a sugar habit. He summed up the regret that has led to tech-free homes across Silicon Valley: "We glimpsed into the chasm of addiction, and there were some lost years, which we feel bad about" (quoted in Bowles, 2018).

Madonna made headlines with a lament that giving her teenagers cellphones "ended my relationship with them ... They became too inundated with imagery and started to compare themselves to other people. And that's really bad for self-growth" (quoted in Aitkenhead, 2019); and renowned sex therapist Dr Ruth expresses concern that "You walk into a restaurant these days, and what you see is everyone with their phone next to them ... Instead of concentrating on the relationship ... they are constantly looking at their phone" (quoted in Hicklin, 2019).

Tech moguls, divas, and popular therapists alike assume smartphone addiction is an individual pathology that savvy parents can address through family-centered remedies and time away from screens. We might wish to be smart like them and engage our children with non-digital substitutes. But what if we are hampered by opportunity costs that render such substitutes unafford-able once we've used up our money – on digital devices?

Individualized solutions for smartphone addiction are available to wealthy families because of their educational, informational, and cultural resources (Greenberg, 2018). Remedies come in a range of settings, from the militarized regimen of the Internet Addiction Treatment Centre in Daxing, China to a breezy tech-free weekend at Camp Grounded in Mendocino, California (West, 2015).[4] Camp Grounded illustrates its wares rather alarmingly, with a photograph of a man shooting a bow

[4] https://campgrounded.org/about/

and arrow, followed by a description of itself as "Pure, Unadulterated Camp For Grown-Ups." We can't wait. But if we *really* can't wait, there's always the "7-Day Phone Breakup Challenge," which promises "a relationship with your phone that actually feels *good*" – and by the way, don't forget to buy the book that tells you how.[5]

The basic business models are similar: teach exercise routines and non-electronic forms of communication until patients aching to touch smartphones and tablets are disciplined, calmed, and ready to return to the world as steadier, and somewhat fitter, consumers. Moderation in all things – apart from phone purchase, of course. Nokia,[6] F(x)tec,[7] and Punkt[8] are onto the possibilities presented by the movement towards a "digital detox." They offer "companion phones" and "entry-level smartphones" with few bells and whistles.

Silicon Valley hegemons' regret at creating addictive technologies reflects an inward-looking egoism that does not translate to the scale of smartphone addiction. If addiction is a social ill that our society confronts with individualized solutions, the wealthy and privileged have a leg up in the quest for healthier digital environ-

[5] https://phonebreakup.com/
[6] https://www.nokia.com/es_int/
[7] https://www.fxtec.com/
[8] https://www.punkt.ch/en/

ments. Their individualized solutions don't make sense for all. They are too expensive, fragmented, and difficult to implement—even budget "digital detox" compounds cost around three hundred dollars a day (Settembre, 2018). (As an alternative, Christian conversion is available by joining Faith Technology's Digital Sabbath.)[9]

The things and rings that keep Bill, Melinda, and Madonna awake at night also worry vast numbers of much poorer people in the Global South, who are concerned about the impact of mobile telephony on children in physical as well as psychological terms (Silver et al., 2019). They need socialized solutions to digital addiction in a manner that serves the greatest number of people – programs that distribute the necessary resources to understand and rival the allure of smartphones. We offer below two existing instances of embracing societal-level methods to reduce risks associated with compulsive cellphone use.

Distracted in Traffic

According to a WHO report, approximately 1.34 million people worldwide die each year in traffic accidents.

[9] https://digitalsabbath.io/

Globally, the chance of being involved in a fatal crash is four times greater for drivers using mobile phones. Texting increases the risk 23 times, while so-called hands-free calling does little to reduce it. Of the countries listed by the WHO, 145 prohibit hand-held phone use, 34 ban hands-free use, and 24 have no relevant legislation (World Health Organization, 2018). In the US, 16 states outlaw talking on cellphones and 47 ban texting while driving (Governors Highway Safety Association, 2018).

The US Department of Transportation (DoT) reports an annual average of 2.3 million people injured in crashes between 2011 and 2015. About 7.5 percent of those accidents were linked to distracted driving, while annual deaths from cellphone distraction averaged about 395 (National Center for Statistics and Analysis, 2017, p. 3, Tables 4 and 6). In 2016, things worsened; 486 people perished in fatal crashes involving cellphone distraction (National Center for Statistics and Analysis, 2018, p. 2, Table 1).[10] European Transport

---

[10] Cellphone distraction as the primary cause of injuries and deaths in traffic accidents may be under-reported, in part because police accident reports "vary across jurisdictions … creating potential inconsistencies in reporting" (National Center for Statistics and Analysis, 2018, p. 4). In addition, unless someone perishes with a phone in their hand, correlations as per driving under the influence of drugs are difficult to establish.

Safety Council statistics indicate that one in ten fatal collisions in France involves a cellphone and one in three in Ireland.[11]

The US spent $186.6 billion per year over the past fifteen years on counterterrorism activities around the world (Mehta, 2018). In 2016, almost 35,000 deaths were attributed to terrorism worldwide, a terrible cost to humanity. But remember those 1.34 million traffic fatalities – numerically a much greater disaster (Ritchie and Roser, 2018). National priorities aimed at protecting lives must invest more to stop the growing problem of distractions on the road (National Center for Statistics and Analysis, 2018, p. 3, Table 5). Fifty years ago, Ralph Nader's book *Unsafe at Any Speed* (1965) was a huge bestseller and started the consumer rights' movement. It pointed out how much car manufacturers knew about road safety – and how little they cared. The controversy it provoked helped create national regulation covering US roads. Something similar is needed to stimulate realism about virtual as well as concrete freeways.

Non-drivers with cellphones in their hands are also at risk. Over the past ten years, there has been

[11] https://etsc.eu/calls-to-increase-education-enforcement-and-pen alties-for-distracted-driving/

an exponential increase of injuries credited to cellphone-using pedestrians walking distractedly into traffic, lampposts, and other people (Jiang et al., 2018; National Safety Council, 2018). We've all irritatedly swerved to avoid the digitally distracted occupying sidewalks without regard for anyone else. After all, what matters to these "smombies [smartphone zombies]" as they are called, is that screen. It might display someone texting to say they've left the library, bought a burger, sold a share, or kissed a cutie. Or perhaps something slightly less earth-shattering, but seemingly noteworthy.

What? I Wasn't Paying Attention

The film *Generation Zapped* (El Gemayel, 2017) documents how people's exposure to radiofrequency radiation increases with cellphone use. Several health experts and scientists are interviewed, one of whom explains that the intensity of radiofrequency and electromagnetic radiation from mobile communication has increased a quintillion times since the arrival of mobile phones, adding for emphasis: "that's a one followed by 18 zeros!" Using academic and personal testimony, the film examines negative health effects linked to exposure to WiFi, cell-tower transmission, smartphones, and other sources of radiofrequency radiation.

When 90 students watched *Generation Zapped* in a class taught by one of us, most responded with startled expressions (and a few with bouts of hypochondria). But there was also a group of impassive faces, ironically aglow from smartphones and laptops. These students turned to their mobile devices and tuned the movie out, staring devotedly at their gadgets throughout.

We are told that young people raised on digital technology can watch a movie, monitor social media, surf the web, conduct a conversation – and comprehend all that content at a high level. When *Zapped* ended, the professor asked students who had been fingering their phones during the screening what the documentary said were the worst places you could put a smartphone and a WiFi-connected laptop. They had no clue (answer: against your ear and on your lap). The professor pointed to the half-dozen WiFi transmitters in the lecture hall to underscore a point made in the movie: exposure to radiofrequency radiation from a wireless device is stronger in such an environment. Most students understood the film's key insights and cautions. But for some in the room, the chance to be enlightened was not as strong an enticement as the light emanating from their smartphones.

The available science shows that cellphones have

a negative impact on learning. For "low-achieving and at-risk students" in school, banning their use is "equivalent to an additional hour a week in school, or to increasing the school year by five days" (Murphy and Beland, 2015). And college? Cornell's renowned "Laptop and the Lecture" study, published in 2003, showed that lecture attendees remembered lessons better if they did not use laptops during class. Subsequent research confirms the risks of technological multitasking with smartphones versus the value of note taking with pen and paper – and not only for those doing so; others get distracted by people typing (Hembrooke and Gay, 2003; Sana et al., 2013).

The research even indicates, paradoxically, that people who engage heavily in media multitasking are worse than others when given multiple tasks to do: sending texts and engaging with social media diminish those capacities, and learning in general (Lawson and Henderson, 2015; Gingerich and Lineweaver, 2014; David et al., 2015; Ophir, Nass, and Wagner, 2009). Similar problems apply to mature-age phone users due to impairment of high-level executive functions such as inhibition and working-memory capacity, which ideally allow us to process temporarily relevant information then let it drop away from our thinking as necessary (Ward et al., 2017; Hartanto and Yang, 2016).

Buzzing Through Us and Messing with Our Natural Vibe

The documentary *Resonance: Beings of Frequency* (Russell, 2013) also covers the potential hazards of cellphones and wireless transmissions. Toward the end of the film, the narrator suggests radiofrequency and electromagnetic radiation may prevent the human body from curing itself of diseases. *Resonance* proposes that mobile technologies threaten the biophysical health of all organisms by disrupting biological processes that have evolved over millions of years. The billions of neurons in our brains use electricity to function and communicate, as do living cells, DNA, genes, and other building blocks of life. This means our neurological systems are intimately related to naturally occurring electromagnetism. In our most relaxed, conscious state, brain waves operate in a frequency range of 8 to 12 Hz – so-called Alpha waves. That's roughly the same fundamental intensity as the Earth's electromagnetic frequency of 7.8 Hz. In other words, our brains have evolved to resonate with planetary electromagnetism (Rusov et al., 2012).

But today, this resonance of body and Earth is jammed by artificial electromagnetic fields (EMF)

(Massey, 1979, p. 149). Manufactured radiofrequency radiation from ubiquitous mobile devices, WiFi, and cell towers have altered our electromagnetic environment on a scale unprecedented in human evolutionary history. As one study of radiation emitted by early model mobile phones put it, "a portable cellular telephone, held in the operating position, will provide a power density of radiofrequency radiation about two billion times greater than occurs naturally in the environment" (Kane, 2001, p. 1).

The WHO explains that EMF surround us "but are invisible to the human eye. Electric fields are produced by the local build-up of electric charges in the atmosphere associated with thunderstorms. The Earth's magnetic field causes a compass needle to orient in a North–South direction and is used by birds and fish for navigation" (World Health Organization, n.d.). A bird's magneto reception works when a cryptochrome photoreceptor protein in its eyes senses the Earth's natural EMF. Disruption of this ability is said to underlie disorders affecting birds and other species (Starr, 2018).

Cryptochrome proteins in humans help synchronize our circadian clocks with solar time. Each of us has a particular chronotype, or internal clock, that tells our bodies the optimal time for sleep to avoid fatigue and illness and permit muscles to rest (Laber-Warren, 2018). Smartphones, tablets, and computer screens emit a blue-light wavelength that tells us it is still daylight, which may interrupt our natural sleep patterns and disrupt the pineal gland's ability to produce melatonin, a hormone with antioxidant properties that is part of our immunological system (Sample, 2018; Li et al., 2017). Antioxidants defend against free radicals, toxic byproducts of oxygen metabolism that can damage cells, including DNA. This is known as oxidative stress (Kivrak et al., 2017; Betteridge, 2000).

The most worrisome breakdown of our bodily defenses concerns illnesses linked to radiofrequency radiation, including damaged DNA, reduced sperm count, oxidative stress, and impaired memory (Environmental Health Trust, n.d.). There are possible links to the proteins that cause Parkinson's and Alzheimer's Diseases (Stefi et al., 2019) and to such autoimmune conditions as multiple sclerosis (Khaki-Khatibi et al., 2019). Exposure to radiation for people living near cellphone base stations is also associated with fatigue, dizziness, poor sleep, headaches, cardiovascular irregularities, poor concentration, depression, diminished prolactin and testosterone, fewer antioxidants, and damaged lymphocytes, *inter alia* (Carlberg et al., 2019). Beyond humans, there is evidence of harm done to vegetables (Chandel et al., 2019) in keeping with what appears to be the capacity of mobile technology's EMF to alter DNA (Panagopoulos, 2019).

The Cancer Question

At the time *Resonance* was made, most scientists considered the studies linking cellphone use to cancer to be inconclusive. Conventional wisdom reflected the warning from the International Agency for Research on Cancer (IARC) that cellphone radiation posed a potential threat and was "possibly carcinogenic to humans" (International Agency for Research on Cancer, 2011). The answer to the cancer question seemed elusive.

In 2016, the US National Toxicology Program (NTP), an interagency initiative of the Department of Health and Human Services, released partial results of a publicly funded study on chronic exposure to cellphone radiation (Wyde et al., 2016). The motivation for the research, which began in 1999, was widespread use of mobile technology and intensified environmental radiation (Wyde et al., pp. 5–6). The preliminary report did not say that cellphones definitively caused cancer in humans, but the authors deemed their results too important to withhold from the public, and opened them to the scientific community for review. There were, of course, caveats acknowledged by the researchers and their evaluators, and plenty of confusing results to work through. But the main point was that this study – the biggest and longest-standing experiment to control for everything but radiofrequency-radiation exposure – generated data that showed apparent causal links between cellphones and cancer. There was great anticipation that the report's final draft would clarify puzzlement associated with the previewed research, once the authors had re-examined their methods, re-analyzed their results, and undergone further extensive peer review by experts in the field.

When a draft final report was released in 2018, the evidence linking cellphone radiation to cancer was still deemed "equivocal" (National Toxicology Program, 2018a). That's one step up from "no evidence" in the NTP's scale. The NTP then convened peer-review panels to assess the methodology and make recommendations on the study's findings (National Toxicology Program, 2018a). The first panel validated the methodology as simulating the effects of cellphone radiation exposure (National Toxicology Program, 2018a, pp. 7–8). The second panel accepted the "conclusions as written" on exposure of mice, which found "equivocal evidence of carcinogenic activity" from Global System for Mobile

Communications (GSM) and Code Division Multiple Access (CDMA)-modulated radiofrequencies (National Toxicology Program, 2018a, p. 20). It came to a different conclusion about rats, recommending an increase of the NTP's level to "clear evidence" of carcinogenic activity in the male heart, and "some evidence" in the male adrenal gland (GSM only) and brain (gliomas) (National Toxicology Program, 2018a, pp. 46–7). It also increased the evidence rating for the female heart (National Toxicology Program, 2018c).

The full study is one of the most expensive and technically complex of its kind (National Institute of Environmental Health Sciences, 2018). The panel's finding of clear evidence that cellphone radiation causes cancer in rats should have been a major media story, especially as another study, published by the Ramazzini Institute in Italy, replicated the NTP's findings on rats the same week (Falcioni et al., 2018; Moskowitz, 2018). The director of research at Ramazzini suggested it was time for IARC to "consider changing the RF radiation designation to a 'probable' human carcinogen" (quoted in Schmidt, 2018, n.p.).

Yet as the *Guardian* noted at the time, "[n]ot one major news organization in the US or Europe reported this scientific news" (Hertsgaard and Dowie, 2018). As we discuss in Chapter 3, the media tend to avoid publicizing scientific studies that do not provide reporters with clear-cut answers to questions of cause and effect. In this case, the focus on rats might have seemed less newsworthy than a conclusive study on humans. Many scientists would disagree, including those who question the results of the NTP study and have used the evidence on female rats to highlight inconsistencies in the NTP results, as well as researchers in South Korea and Japan, who plan to carry out their own tests with rats to see if they can replicate the NTP findings.[12]

As with all ongoing scientific work, significant "peer review and professional challenges" will ensue (Mann and Toles, 2016, p. 1). It's part of the scientific process to take seriously evidence that challenges preconceptions. But in the words of the former NTP senior toxicologist who helped design the research, "it's unlikely any future study could conclude with certainty that there is no risk to humans from cellphone use" (Schlanger, 2018, n.p.). The phrase "any future study" implies that science is still working on the answer. The layperson might interpret that as a sign not to worry. But the point of the NTP research was to find out whether simulated cellphone radiation could produce cancerous

[12] https://microwavenews.com/news-center/japan-korea-ntp-rf-pro ject

tumors. As one panelist noted, it sought to "test the null hypothesis. People were saying, 'this is non-ionizing radiation, there's no possibility of adverse biological effect,' and therefore the study was designed to challenge that hypothesis" (National Toxicology Program, 2018b, p. 13). Like the Ramazzini group, the NTP concluded that adverse effects are possible. The next step is for scientific studies to find the biological mechanisms that may cause cancer, which will explain the likely risks to humans from radiofrequency radiation. Until then, doubts will overshadow the NTP research – but not of the kind that has been generated by the phone and telecom industries and their scholarly scions (Melnick, 2019).

The NTP and Ramazzini studies challenge the expectations of scholars who subscribe to the null hypothesis, that wireless and cellphone radiation is benign. As *Newsweek* put it, "[s]cientists have clung to one reassuring point: According to everything we know about physics and biology, cellphones should not cause cancer. The radio waves they emit are 'nonionizing,' meaning they don't damage our DNA the way ultraviolet light from the sun or X-rays do" (Cohen, 2018). This powerful idea encourages many in the scientific community to sideline research that links radiofrequency radiation to health risks (q.v. Grimes, 2018).

Finally, various political-economic forces want this research suppressed. The US wireless and telecommunications industry has inordinate power to define the health risks of cellphones. It has accumulated cellphone usage data over decades, but refuses to release the information for academic scrutiny (Cohen, 2018). CTIA is the industry's powerful peak body. It filed suit against the cities of San Francisco and Berkeley when they passed "right to know" ordinances to warn shoppers of the risks of radiofrequency radiation exposure when carrying mobile phones in their pockets, pants, or bras. San Francisco gave up its effort after losing in the federal appeals court. CTIA argues that the warnings violate cellphone merchants' free speech rights, which US Supreme Court Justice Kagan called "weaponizing the First Amendment" against "workaday economic and regulatory policy" (quoted in Peeples, 2018) that merely summarized the FCC's mandated disclosure of radiofrequency risks mentioned in the Introduction. Berkeley is still battling the CTIA (Gupta, 2018). Meanwhile, the CTIA's policy positions on what it terms "Public Safety" simply exclude health risks from its pet devices.[13]

Clearly, the CTIA does not want the public to think

---

[13] https://www.ctia.org/positions/911-public-safety

about possible risks. That's also evident in the tens of millions of dollars it has spent lobbying the federal government over the last decade (Center for Responsive Politics, 2018). FCC guidelines on radiofrequency radiation exposure have not changed since the mid-1990s, when the Commission established safe levels based on SAR by testing simulated exposure on a model originally designed in the 1950s using an average of male army soldiers' heads and bodies; SAR levels have never accounted for children's or women's risks from exposure. As noted in the Introduction, the FCC does not independently test for SAR levels, leaving the industry to police itself (Alster, 2015).

The US Food and Drug Administration (FDA) advises the FCC on setting guidelines after reviewing available research. But after the initial draft of the NTP study was announced, the FDA did not instruct the FCC to change its safety guidelines (Shuren, 2018). Research across the decades and continents confirms that this complacent, cozy conflict of interests is neither new nor unusual (Pockett, 2019).

Meanwhile, the IARC warns that cellphone frequencies are "possibly carcinogenic to humans." The US National Cancer Institute continues to hold that, while studies have not proven cellphones cause cancer, additional research is needed because technologies change so quickly. And the American Academy of Pediatrics presses the FCC and the FDA to revise EMF standards to account for different people's vulnerability to cancer from cellphones, notably pregnant women and children (McInerney, 2013; Wall et al., 2019). If there is any chance of health risks from using cellphones, we should continue to act with caution – use wired headphones, text, and speakerphone, and keep phones away from head and body as much as possible. Outsmart your smartphone.

5G and the Internet of Things – The Smog of Radiation

All the above presents a worrisome prelude to the seemingly inevitable deployment of Fifth Generation (5G) wireless technology, which will increase radiofrequency and electromagnetic radiation. In the name of technological progress, the telecommunications industry is poised to build an extensive network of 5G transmitters in the service of a new regime of internet-enabled devices – the Internet of Things (TechRepublic, n.d.). The industry's full-court press for 5G technologies via advertising and marketing campaigns is breathtaking. It promises an ever-denser digital environment of smart wearable computers, cellphones, and mobile devices, inexorably amplifying connectedness between people and electronic things, as well as thing-to-thing communication.

We know next to nothing about 5G radiation and health risks, because there has been no significant pre-market research, other than studies sponsored by the industry (Environmental Health Trust, n.d.). It doesn't seem to matter that our bodies are being pushed into an uncontrolled wireless experiment minus our informed consent. While 5G has a weaker energy output relative to prior wireless transmission systems, it uses a higher frequency and can only travel a short distance. That means its antennae must be close to one another and to people. Over two hundred and forty scientists and physicians (the list is growing) have called for a moratorium on 5G because of the potential health risks posed by adding radiation to 2-, 3-, and 4G systems (5G Appeal, 2017; Canadians for Safe Technology, n.d.). In the words of Joel Moskowitz, director of the Center for Family and Community Health at the University of California, Berkeley, "people will be bathed in a smog of radiation 24/7" (quoted in Hertsgaard and Dowie, 2018b). And our legal protections? For now, the widespread use and adoration of smartphones and the networks that interconnect them give the telecom-

"If there is any chance of health risks from using cellphones, we should continue to act with caution."

munications industry and their lobbyists leverage in Washington D. C. – where all their wishes, so far, have come true (Hertsgaard and Dowie, 2018b). It doesn't have to be that way. Examples from around the world demonstrate we are smart enough not to tolerate this situation.

Precautionary Principle

Health agencies throughout the European Union and elsewhere have issued warnings based on scientific studies of cellphone and wireless risks, even as research is ongoing (Parents for Safe Technology, n.d.). This "better safe than sorry" guideline is known as the precautionary principle, which was outlined in the Introduction: if we don't know a technology will not harm us, we shouldn't use it. If there is any evidence of potential harm, we must act as if confronting real and present dangers. Caution first. We won't be damned by smartphones as we were in the previous century by lead and tobacco (Michaels, 2019).

In the Introduction we also learned about "phone-gate," the revelations from the French ANFR study that most "phones exceed government radiation limits" (Environmental Health Trust, 2018). Based on this research and a strong commitment to the precautionary principle, the ANFR has pursued an aggressive campaign to recall phones and pressure manufacturers to ensure safer levels of exposure (Agence Nationale des Fréquences, n.d.).

Our smartphones conceal the potential hazards of addiction, distraction, radiofrequency radiation, and EMFs. We could design smartphones to contribute to our health and help, rather than hinder, our ability to relate as ecosystem inhabitants. In the meantime, we must do our best with what the industry produces, which may not be welcome news for smartphone merchants. As our next chapter shows, the greenest smartphone is the one you already own.

TWO

The Greenest Smartphone is the One You Already Own

Smartphones can last well beyond their warranties. But most of us get rid of them after less than two years (Britons hold on to theirs for 23.5 months, Americans for 21.6). The reason is rarely to do with replacing a broken phone or one that can't run the latest software. Not even planned obsolescence is a clear culprit, because most phones are designed for a longer life than consumers allow. We choose newer models because we are promised slightly faster processing, better cameras, or improved data security. Comparing our existing phone to new ones, the thing in our hands fails to be state-of-the-art; it's no longer cool (Baldé et al., 2018, pp. 20–1).

Most household appliances such as freezers and washers last a decade and more. Their breakdowns can generally be repaired for much less than the cost of replacement ("By the Numbers," 2009; Lawrence, 2019). Imagine if we threw these items away because they had lost their cool factor! Our societies would be inundated with electronic and electric garbage. That's precisely what happens when we discard our smart-phones so frequently, regardless of their functionality. We're helping to bury our planet under mountains of e-waste because of our enchantment with the new – that damned technological sublime (Baldé et al., 2018, p. 20).

With each fevered purchase of a new smartphone, we also increase carbon emissions. That's because of the electricity and petroleum required for manufacturing and transporting smartphones, tablets, and other electronics. (Though by contrast with other digital devices, smartphones use a modest amount of electricity over their lifetimes.) Our penchant for buying new phones also sets in motion a chain of events that reaches across the planet to the mines and factories where smartphones are made. The hazards and despair that characterize workers' lives in those locations intensify whenever we place orders for the latest model. For all these reasons, the greenest smartphone is the one you already own. After looking into the energy required to make and use these devices, this chapter examines four moments in their life cycles to illustrate why holding on to them for as long as possible is best for our planet and the people who make and disassemble them.

Energy Consumption and Carbon Emissions

Until recently, most studies of smartphones' energy consumption and greenhouse-gas emissions predicted a growing carbon footprint, linking that growth to increased data traffic and surges in mobile telecommunications. It was common to see headlines declaring that "*Smartphones Are Killing the Planet Faster Than Anyone Expected*" (Wilson, 2018). That one, from the business magazine *Fast Company*, was based on widely circulated research that projected ominous consequences from our continued love affair with smartphones (Belkhir and Elmeligi, 2018).

Worrisome examples abounded: one hour of video streaming to an individual mobile device via the cloud used more electricity than two new refrigerators (Mills, 2013); the International Energy Agency (IEA) estimated that US$80 billion was wasted on powering mobile devices in 2014 when in standby mode – more than Canada's annual energy use (2014); the Carbon Trust showed that people watching football via mobile telephony multiplied their footprint tenfold in comparison with television or WiFi signals (Carbon Trust, n.d.; Carbon Trust, 2016).

The energy powering consumer electronics worldwide

"With each fevered purchase of a new smartphone, we also increase carbon emissions."

had reached 15 percent of residential electricity use in 2009, and was on target to reach 30 percent of global energy demand by 2022, and 45 percent by 2030 (Smith, 2010; Mouawad and Galbraith, 2009; International Energy Agency 2009: 5, 21; Climate Group 2008: 18–23; Hancock, 2009; Organization for Economic Co-Operation and Development 2010: 19; Greenpeace, 2012). In 2013, reports estimated that 90 percent of the total energy consumed by mobile connection was attributable to wireless access providers – not counting the energy used by the devices themselves. Another nine percent was linked to data-center energy use (Centre for Energy-Efficient Telecommunications et al., 2013).

But predictions of ever-dirtier information and communications technologies (ICT) have been too dire, as we now see slower increases in energy consumption through mobile phones, even as data traffic has risen (Malmodin and Lundén, 2018). While the preconditions for such positive changes vary from country to country, depending on the national electricity mix, recent efforts to aggregate and analyze communication carbon footprints have found greener trends than anticipated (Höjer, Eriksson, and Preist, 2018).

In 2018, Swedish researchers examined five years of global data on the energy use and carbon footprint of

ICT and entertainment media (EM) (Malmodin and Lundén, 2018, pp. 28–9). They found that the ICT portion of the electronic media's global carbon footprint was 1.4 percent in 2015, about the same as 2010 levels. Data centers and business networks accounted for 22 percent and ICT networks 24 percent. Fifty-four percent came from user devices (this includes embodied carbon from manufacturing and transport and carbon emissions from electricity consumption over the lifetime of the gadgetry). The EM portion (excluding cinemas, theaters, and other exhibitionary sites) was 1.2 percent of the global total, of which two-thirds was produced by television sets, networks, and consumer electronics and the rest by print media and home and business printers. Overall, the EM carbon footprint declined as technology became more energy-efficient and consumers turned to smartphones. Diminished use of PCs and TVs has meant "large energy savings," as smaller devices need less electricity. A smartphone's carbon footprint is highest during its extractive, manufacturing, and transport phases (embodied carbon), though still low by contrast with televisions, desktop computers, and laptops (Malmodin and Lundén, 2018, p. 18).

Meanwhile, the study notes that "data traffic (mobile and WiFi) from smartphones has grown fast from <1% in 2010 to about 10% in 2015 and will continue to grow fast to about 30–40% in 2020" (Malmodin and Lundén, 2018, p. 16). The expansion of video and streaming services is increasing demand for storage and high-speed processing in data centers. This raises the specter of the dirty cloud and its carbon footprint; but here, too, the latest research is showing improvements in emissions and electricity use. Data centers' electricity consumption and carbon emissions were supposed to increase exponentially with the rise in data traffic. Indeed, Greenpeace estimated in 2012 that the level of data centers' electricity consumption around the world was somewhere between the amount of energy India and Japan used annually. They predicted it would continue to grow at a rapid pace (Greenpeace International, 2012). That hasn't happened.

The Swedish researchers found that while global data traffic increased about "30 times over 2005–2015," the "computing capacity per amount of energy for a typical one socket rack server has increased 100-fold over 2005–2015" (Malmodin and Lundén, 2018, p. 11). The IEA has confirmed that data centers' average global electricity consumption stabilized after 2010 and predicts that it will remain relatively stable to 2020 (International Energy Agency, 2017, pp. 105–6). A study conducted for the US Department of Energy found that in the US, which has about a third of the world's data-center market, electricity use by data centers stopped growing in 2010 and remained at about 1.8 percent of total national consumption through 2014 (Shehabi et al., 2016, p. 1). This trend is due to efficiency improvements, without which data centers' electricity consumption would have doubled over the period (International Energy Agency, 2017, p. 105).

Not all data centers perform at sustainable levels. There are problems to overcome, especially in smaller configurations (the vast majority) and countries with a dirty electricity mix. However, the Swedish study cites evidence that the ICT sector represents over 50 percent of corporate "renewable power purchasing agreements (PPAs)." Even if we lowered this number to account for biases in corporate self-reporting, the authors tell us that the "ICT sectors' actual usage [of PPAs] is probably higher compared to other sectors" (Malmodin and Lundén, 2018, p. 14).

Newer technologies and the emergence of "hyperscale" data centers have presented models for ongoing improvements in energy consumption. Hyperscale data centers have begun to replace smaller, localized, less-efficient systems. One server in a hyperscale data center can replace 3.75 servers in non-hyperscale locations (Shehabi et al., 2016, p. 36; Hussain et al., 2019). The emergence of fog and edge computing, where information is located closer to users than is the case with clouds, promises a greener solution (Buyya and Srirama, 2019).

But the environmental potential of these centers can be stifled. Barriers to a full "hyperscale shift" include concerns with security and regulation (Shehabi et al., 2016, p. 46) and resistance from industries where instant data transmission is critical. In the financial sector, for example, milliseconds count (Lewis, 2014; Zook and Grote, 2017). Existing hyperscale data centers are located too far from flash traders to deliver real-time transmission (Aswani, 2016). Policy reformers looking at the financial sector would do well to consider the environmental impact of data centers built for such purposes (Krugman, 2014, p. A23). And as more businesses move to the cloud, it's important to keep in mind that data centers must be held to a high standard for their electricity consumption and carbon footprint (Pearce, 2018).

Wireless telecommunications are more energy-intensive than landline technology, but the difference is diminishing: 2G networks are over a hundred times more energy-intensive than fixed-line networks, 3G networks more than ten times, and 4G networks about four times. Network improvements help reduce the rate of increase, but higher speeds may create a rebound effect of higher usage, off-setting overall reductions in electricity usage (Shehabi et al., 2016, pp. 41–4).

As we learnt in Chapter 1, the next mobile network based on 5G technology could increase human exposure to radiofrequency radiation. And there are additional problems with 5G. The so-called fiber backhaul – the fixed-wired backbone of low latency, high data-rate mobile wireless – is poorly developed in the US and UK (the latter a distinct laggard) especially in rural areas. Without the necessary fiber infrastructure, the promised speed and features of the Internet of Things will be unevenly distributed, perhaps deepening existing digital divides. As the consulting firm Deloitte suggests, "limited competition" between oligopolistic telecom companies provides little incentive to upgrade inefficient infrastructure (2017, p. 11). There are no national regulatory incentives to improve infrastructure. Public policy has essentially released these corporations from public-service obligations to make data transmission networks green, affordable, and reliable – though on a local scale, many US cities targeted for 5G networks have resisted telecommunications firms seeking to take over the urban landscape (International Telecommunications Union, 2018b, p. 17). And what about the workers?

Eighty years ago, the noted playwright, dramaturg, and poet Bertolt Brecht posed "A Worker's Question While Reading," a moving paean to labor (1935). Brecht's question concerned those who have shaped history but are left out of it, excluded from written records. His poem juxtaposes leading figures of conventional history with a query about those who enabled their successes but are forgotten. Brecht asks: "Every 10 years a great man. Who paid the bill?" What, we wonder, would "A Consumer's Question While Texting" reveal about what happens beyond the subject position of the consummate consumer of smartphones. Perhaps it might be: "Every two years a new model. Who paid the bill?"

The reality is that blood, sweat, and tears are embodied in cellphones. They come from workers who successively mine the metals that make smartphone magic, produce its enchanting components, and wipe away any trace of such labor. We turn now to the labor process, from extracting the minerals that go into cellphones, notably conflict minerals, through to manufacturing. Then we consider the impact on these processes of prevailing business models, concluding with a look at how smartphones contribute to the global catastrophe of e-waste.

"The reality is that blood, sweat, and tears are embodied in cellphones."

The Labor Process Part 1:
Mining Hazards and Conflict Minerals

Seventy stable (non-radioactive) elements from the periodic table are present in smartphones. Copper, gold, platinum, silver, and tungsten are the main metals in basic microelectronic components, wires, and solder. Aluminum and cobalt are used in casings and batteries. Numerous rare-earth metals enhance smartphone functions in speakers and microphones, from signature vibrations to brilliant colors (Crowston, 2018, p. 9; Jardim, 2017, p. 4).

Mining these metals is hazardous for workers in Asia, Africa, South America, and locations where ores are exported for processing. They are exposed to respiratory hazards and radioactive elements, often in countries where the industry is unregulated or laws are poorly enforced. Miners frequently work on unstable terrain or in vulnerable underground sites where they confront combustible dust, fires, and mine collapses. Breathing ore dust can lead to lung diseases, including bronchitis, silicosis, and cancer. Gold-mining byproducts include such poisonous neurotoxins as lead, cyanide, and mercury (Grossman, 2016, pp. 67–8).

Some metals used in smartphones – gold (for

circuitry), tin (for solder), tungsten (for capacitors aiding vibration), and tantalum (capacitors for audio) – are known as "conflict minerals." They mostly derive from the Democratic Republic of Congo (DRC) and have funded the country's ongoing civil war, in which millions of lives have been lost. While there is some evidence of demilitarization over the last five years in eastern DRC, armed groups continue to profit from mines, which they control through violence, sexual abuse, and rape, working alongside dozens of Chinese and Indian companies – all merrily profiting from a workforce laden with thousands of pre-teen children ("Progress and Challenges of Conflict Minerals," 2018; United States Government Accountability Office 2018; Kara, 2018; Scheele et al., 2016). Anyone wishing to hear the voices of those suffering from this brutal industry can view numerous documentaries and reports that provide chilling testimony (*Conflicted*, 2019; *Conflict Minerals*, 2012; *Special Report*, 2017; *Congo*, 2011).

But in general, these crimes are highlighted much more than the overall political economy of the labor process and its toxicity, both of which are kept far-distant from smartphone owners (Laudati and Mertens, 2019). They focus on the health and psychological impacts of cellphones on their own families rather than the broken and contaminated bodies of enslaved children, whose invisible labor is crucial to their First-World worries (Gallagher, 2019).

Major US electronics manufacturers continue to profit from the trade, despite having pledged to abide by the Dodd–Frank Wall Street Reform and Consumer Protection Act, which prohibits obtaining these minerals from the DRC. Due diligence and support for "conflict-free sourcing opportunities" are good things, but companies down the line still can't be confident they are buying conflict-free minerals, because it is notoriously difficult to ascertain the origins of these metals: once processed, ore is mixed with the overall global supply, then sold on the international market (Callaway, 2017). The European Union has legislation designed to stem the trade, but it only applies to firms that are direct importers and hence will have little if any effect on the phone business (van den Brink et al., 2019).

The Labor Process Part 2: Manufacturing and Assembly

> *I work like a machine and my brain is rusted.* – 19-year old female worker from Guangxi at the

Compeq printed circuit board factory in Huizhou City, China (quoted in Chan and Ho, 2008, p. 22)

There are many good reasons to share stories about the hardships faced by workers who extract minerals and labor in the factories that supply the world with smartphones. The most obvious is that a compelling account of hidden labor can open our eyes to the human origins of our devices,. Of course, that doesn't just apply to electronics: we rarely think about the origins of our soap, clothes, or cars; they seemingly appear in retail outlets fully formed, without any outward sign of their histories. But billions of electronic gadgets arrive with a toxic pedigree that most of us never hear about. So it is a healthy reminder that somewhere, someone, makes the things we need and want.

The production of silicon wafers, semiconductors, batteries, and other basic components in smartphones involve exposure to toxic chemicals. "Solvents – such as benzene, glycol ethers, methylene chloride, trichloroethylene (TCE), trichlorethane, acetone, toluene – acids, heavy metals and perfluorinated compounds are among the many hazardous chemicals used in producing semiconductors" (Grossman, 2016, p. 70; also see Kim, Kim, and Paek, 2014). They have been linked to brain and kidney disorders, brain cancers, leukemia, and lymphoma. Other chemicals used to manufacture smartphones are associated with reproductive disorders, infertility, miscarriages, and birth defects. Many such diseases do not manifest themselves for years. The industry only reports harms that occur at work, so the statistics underreport health risks facing workers and their families (Grossman, 2016, p. 71). Data from Norwegian silicon-carbide smelters indicate elevated risks of stomach and lung cancer by contrast with the wider population, as a consequence of exposure to crystalline silica, dust fibres, and silicon carbide (Romundstad et al., 2001).

In 2015, workers in South Korea and elsewhere in the world's electronics factories were contracting leukemia, lymphoma, breast cancer, brain tumors, and ovarian cancer while making computer chips and flat screens for our phones and TVs (Sung-Won, 2019). Well over two hundred cases of diseases that interfere with blood-clotting "have been reported among relatively young people who have worked in Samsung's semi-conductor, LCD, mobile phone and other chemically intensive manufacturing plants" (Grossman, 2016, p. 71).

Most component manufacture and smartphone assembly takes place in east Asia; 57 percent of smartphone exports originate from China (Jardim, 2017, p. 5). Research on conditions in factories throughout

the region finds that workers receive little or no training in the safe handling of "chemicals that include
phenol, chloroform, TCE, mercury, glues, solvents,
flux and solder, degreaser, hexane, n-hexane, methanol,
trimethyl fluoride, benzene, nickel, lithium, methylene
chloride, and isopropyl alcohol" (Grossman, 2016, pp.
71–2).

Investigations into Apple's Chinese suppliers have
shown that the corporation has been aware of its subcontractors' unsafe and illegal operations for years (Maxwell
and Miller, 2012, p. 95). At the Lian Jian Technology
Group in the eastern city of Suzhou (owned by the
Taiwanese firm Wintek) 137 workers were poisoned by
the chemical n-hexane while preparing iPhone touch-
screens. N-hexane poisoning damages the peripheral
nervous system, which is extremely painful and leads
to numbness in the limbs, chronic weakness, fatigue,
and hypersensitivity to heat and cold. Workers suffering
from n-hexane poisoning at the factory wrote to Jobs for
help, asking, "When you look down at the Apple phone
you are using in your hand and you swipe it with your
finger is it possible that you can feel as if it is no longer a
beautiful screen to show off but the life and the blood of
us employees and victims?" Jobs never replied (quoted
in Maxwell and Miller, 2012, p. 157).

Apple also acted indifferently to the searing

conditions behind mass suicides in 2010–11 at the Chinese Foxconn factory making iPhones. Foxconn Technology Group, a transnational Taiwanese corporation, controls over half the global market in electronics manufacturing. If you own a smartphone, the chances are it was assembled by Foxconn in China. For almost twenty years after setting up there, the firm "evaded its legal responsibility to establish a trade union." When it took steps to do so in 2006–7, CEO Terry Gou put one of his personal assistants in charge. After the first spate of suicides at Foxconn's high-rise factory dormitories in 2010, the union leader refused to investigate workplace causes, remarking only that "suicide is foolish, irresponsible and meaningless." Another six suicide attempts followed, and there would be over two dozen deaths that year. The company responded with self-help seminars and an emergency hot line for workers. It also increased automation, built new factories in low-wage interior regions of China, and routinely failed to pay employees for overtime, while actively manipulating health and pension plans to deny them money and benefits (Chan et al., 2016).

Apple finally responded in its 2011 annual supply chain audit by welcoming improved wages, safety measures, and counseling services at Foxconn. The corporation also acknowledged the poisonings at the

Lian Jian factory and other code-of-conduct violations, including the employment of underage girls by some subcontractors. But although Apple ordered its subcontractors to halt unsafe and illegal practices, company representatives kept their distance, never meeting with affected workers or offering support, financial or otherwise, to rehabilitate or compensate them for physical and emotional privation (Chan et al., 2016).

Suicides at these plants point to the brutality of twenty-first-century electronics manufacturing combining with mass mobilization of rural Chinese youth – perhaps the largest migration in history, and certainly the most vigorous peacetime activation of a reserve army of labor (Gong, 2019; Pun, Tse, and Ng, 2019). In the words of one factory manager: "There are ... plenty of girls with good eyes and strong hands. If we run out of people, we just go deeper into China" (quoted in Catholic Agency for Overseas Development, 2004, p. 31).

Manufacturers like Foxconn have implemented an inhumane system that some social scientists have characterized as a new form of slavery (Qiu, 2016). The system removes young people from family, friends, freedom of association (they are prohibited from talking to one another on the assembly line) and forms of cultural enjoyment and release, which might help them adjust to sequestration in high-tech, high-speed, high-security compounds. Working days can be as long as twelve hours, with overtime to follow. Stress levels are high, and repetitive motion and other ergonomic problems common (Lu, 2019). Because many workers are on short-term contracts, it is "difficult for them to become informed about their working conditions, difficult for them to organize, [and] difficult to trace workplace exposures and … any resulting health problems" (Grossman, 2016, p. 72). Again, you can view testimony from those on the front line of this abuse (Qiu, 2010; *Made in China*, 2017). Meanwhile, watch Gou's trajectory: in 2019, he announced that the Buddhist-Taoist sea goddess Mazu had urged him in a dream to stand for the presidency of Taiwan (Wu, 2019). And note that he has been described by Donald Trump as "one of the great businessmen of our time" (quoted in Horton, 2019)

The semiconductor, the heart of all electronic equipment, is produced by hundreds of companies around the world for a market dominated by Intel, Samsung Electronics, Toshiba Electronics, Texas Instruments, Qualcomm, and ADM. A single semiconductor facility may require 832 million cubic feet of bulk gases, 5.72 million cubic feet of hazardous gases, 591 million gallons of deionized water, 5.2 million pounds of chemicals, including acids and solvents, and 8.8 million kilowatt hours of electrical power. Workers can be exposed to skin irritants, acids that harm mucous and pulmonary tissue, and chemicals that may cause cancer, reproductive complications, and debilitating illnesses. The durable half-life of toxic waste emitted into the soil from semiconductor plants leaves groundwater and land unusable or highly dangerous for populations who live atop them long after culpable firms have departed. Entire communities like Endicott, New York – the original home of IBM – have seen their aquifer and soil cursed with such carcinogenic compounds as trichloroethylene (a solvent) that will remain active for decades (Silicon Valley Toxics Coalition, n.d.; Grossman, 2006, pp. 109–11).

The Labor Process Part 3: The Business Model

The 2014 study *Dragging Out the Best Deal: How Billion Dollar Margins Are Played Out on the Backs of Electronics Workers* revealed how the business model that brands like Apple pioneered has solidified the behavior of subcontractors like Foxconn (Harris, 2014). Rules are in place to ensure a percentage mark-up of price at each stage, from factory floor to retail store. That encourages inflexible workplace conditions.

At the start of the supply chain, the contract manufacturer selling price combines assembly costs (including labor) and materials costs (determined by the brand company) plus a small profit – usually no more than three percent of the factory-selling price. Apple and its kind are assured a price mark-up of 30 percent to pay for "development, shipping, distribution, marketing." They may add a further 30 percent as profit. Such mark-ups compound price increases at each stage up to the retailer's cut, taxes, and internet-provider contracts. In the end, the total price for a smartphone or other gadget can be five times or more than the contract manufacturer's selling point (Harris, 2014). Factory labor costs in this example amount to about 0.5 percent of the final retail price, meaning that the total amount paid for workers to make a $500 device is about $2. That's not $2 for each employee; it's the collective share for all the labor incarnate in the device.

As a consequence of this business model, companies like Foxconn have little incentive to raise wages or improve working conditions. Their profit margins are small, though they can finagle increased revenue from suppliers without increasing their selling price. Proprietors therefore hold wages down and speed up the pace of work. High pressure on workers is a feature designed into this supply chain, created for Apple by Cook (Isaacson, 2011, pp. 360–1).

Dragging Out the Best Deal tells a story of Apple abruptly demanding a change of screens on the first iPhones. Foxconn rousted 8,000 workers out of bed in the middle of the night, gave them tea and biscuits, and within thirty minutes pressed them into an unexpected twelve-hour shift. Foxconn ramped up production over four days until 10,000 units with new screens were finished per day (Harris, 2014, pp. 6–9). This rapacious exploitation cost Apple nothing and earned it millions.

Faced with a political economy that condones such a business model, we need solidarity between electronics workers and digital consumers (see resources in the Conclusion). Because we're smarter than smartphones, we can eliminate the estrangement between worker and consumer, look for the political and economic ties that bind us, and make ethical commitments to electronics workers based in mutuality, justice, and equality. Such commitments must stretch across the global supply chain.

The alternative to such solidarity is the status quo: profits beaten out of the lives of employees, while we pay a premium for smartphones to feed those profits still more. It's time to ask Apple to pay good wages directly to the workers who make our smartphones.

Trust us, it won't go broke. The company is valued at a trillion dollars (La Monica, 2018).

The Labor Process Part 4: Our Global E-Waste Problem

What happens when we decide our smartphones have had their day? Smartphones fall into an e-waste category of small ICT equipment that includes Global Positioning Systems (GPS), pocket calculators, routers, personal computers, printers, and telephones (Baldé et al., 2018, p. 11). They also overlap with monitors, televisions, laptops, notebooks, and tablets. Discarding these devices creates large quantities of waste, but measuring it reliably is notoriously difficult. According to a joint study by the UNU and the ITU, only 20 percent of the numbers come from fully documented e-waste that has been designated for recycling. The remaining 80 percent is a statistical projection drawn from sales, trade volume and weight, and the average lifespan of equipment (Baldé et al., 2018, pp. 30–5). Compounding the measurement problem is the fact that one-third of the world's population live where there is no e-waste legislation, and only 41 countries produce official e-waste statistics. The fate of undocumented waste is uncertain.

Researchers assume it is dumped in landfills or recycled in low-tech, high-hazard conditions. Our best estimate is that screens, small ITCs, and larger telecommunications devices account for just over ten percent of total e-waste globally, which is about 46 to 50 million metric tons. That figure is growing by three to four percent a year (Baldé et al., 2018, pp. 39–40).

If we index these smaller digital devices to e-waste in general, we find that the most discarded cellphone waste per capita is produced in Asia, and the least in Africa. China holds the top spot for overall e-waste production, while North America, the European Union, and Oceania have the highest amounts per capita. The latter is mostly due to Australia's high level, because the rest of the region produces the lowest amount per person (Baldé et al., 2018, p. 68).

Most digital waste produced in the US is probably sent to Asia for recycling or dumping (Baldé et al., 2018, p. 44). Precise data on the flow is as murky as the overall e-waste picture. US recyclers claim that most documented e-waste is recycled locally (Public Broadcasting Service, 2016). But the Basel Action Network (BAN) has revealed a disturbing trend of "export denial in the recycling industry" (2016). This research was based on evidence from radio tracking devices BAN installed in electronics that it delivered to certified US recyclers, which disclosed that 40 percent of the tracked e-waste had been dispatched overseas, nearly all of it illegally.

The export of waste containing toxic materials is regulated by the *Basel Convention on the Control of Transboundary Movements of Hazardous Wastes and Their Disposal*, which was adopted in 1989 and ratified three years later. The Convention imposes strict rules on transporting and handling e-waste, and even stricter ones limiting or prohibiting its export to the Global South. It is illegal for any signatory to receive e-waste from the US – the only wealthy country that has refused to sign (Basel Convention, 1989).

Until 2017, China was the final resting home for 70 percent of the world's e-waste, much of it ending up in landfills, sub-standard treatment sites, and low-tech salvage yards. New restrictions have reduced imports, as the PRC deals with its internal burden of waste management. As a consequence, e-waste is shifting to smaller Asian countries where merchants dump overflow (Larmer, 2018). Nevertheless, a portion of e-waste still ends up in mainland China after arriving in Hong Kong as an *entrepôt*, while much of the remainder finds its way to Pakistan, Thailand, Taiwan, Cambodia, United Arab Emirates, Togo, and Kenya. The big change over the last quarter of a century is the massive intra-Asian trade in e-waste, such is the growth of middle-class norms of disposability in China and India (Lepawsky, 2015).

The European Union leads the world in e-waste collection and recycling, but is far from innocent of illegal exports to the Global South. Much of the Union's electronic waste goes to Asia and West Africa, specifically Benin, Côte d'Ivoire, Ghana, Liberia, and Nigeria. Ghana and Nigeria are the main regional ports of entry for e-waste from around the world. Over three-quarters coming into Nigeria originates in Europe, most of it smuggled inside motor vehicles that have been shipped as "roll on/roll off" cargo to Lagos (Shaw 2019; Odeyingbo, Nnorom, and Deubzer, 2017, p. 36; Gault, 2018).

There is a dreadful human cost to these illegal shipments, visible in such documentaries as *Electronic Waste in Ghana* (2008) and *ToxiCity* (2016).

As we have seen, smartphones contain a range of toxic components that can cause human and ecological damage. Recyclers in the informal sector (ragpickers) generally operate beyond taxation, labor laws, and police, collecting, separating, cataloguing, and selling materials from spurned consumer and business products that have made their way to rubbish dumps and low-income areas. Most ragpickers do not earn wages from employers; nor are they in registered co-operatives or small businesses. The health risks they run include brain damage, headaches, vertigo, nausea, birth defects, diseases of the bones, stomach, lungs, and other vital organs, and disrupted biological development in children. These conditions result from exposure to heavy metals (lead, cadmium, chromium, and mercury) burned plastics, and poisonous, often carcinogenic, fumes emitted when melting components in search of precious metals (United Nations University/StEP Initiative, 2016). Indian ragpickers, who number in the hundreds of thousands, suffer an historically unprecedented prevalence of low hemoglobin, high monocyte and eosinophil counts, gum disease, diarrhea, and dermatitis. In Brazil, where it's estimated that there are half a million ragpickers, extraordinary levels of physiological disorder and psychological distress are reported (Maxwell and Miller, 2012).

There are also huge ecosystem risks from low-tech, high-hazard recycling of e-waste. Plastics are a particularly pernicious problem in e-waste treatment, because the flame retardants, toxic elements, and heavy metals used in their production can release hazardous chemicals into the environment and food chain if not properly recycled (Wäger, Schluep, and Müller, 2010; Beurteaux, 2018).

Consider the recent history of Guiyu, a village in

south-eastern China. Once a farming area, 80 percent of local families left farming behind in favor of more remunerative e-waste recycling. Contaminants from that recycling saturated the human food chain, and persistent organic pollutants in the soil and water prohibited the safe return of affected agricultural lands to future generations. After worldwide publicity of this disaster, thanks largely to BAN, the Chinese authorities restricted illegal dumping and foreign imports of scrap into Guiyu, confining e-waste processing to a new industrial park ("Chinese City," 2015). The tragedy is that even if Guiyu returned to agricultural production, the odds are it could only produce poisoned crops ("In Guiyu," 2016).

Smartphones contain precious and rare-earth metals and recyclable plastics as well as recoverable metals like iron and aluminum. A Swiss study showed that while critical metals like neodymium and indium are found in small quantities, they provide key functions to digital devices: indium tin oxide is electrically conductive and transparent, making it a key material in screens, and neodymium is used for the magnets in speakers (Thiébaud et al., 2018, n.p.).

There are very few government incentives to manage e-waste transparently and legally, despite estimates that the recovery of high-value components through the formal economy could be worth as much as $63 billion (Baldé et al., 2018, p. 54). As the UNU/ITU report puts it, from a "resource perspective for secondary raw materials of e-waste," the potential value for high-tech, low hazard recycling would amount to "more than the 2016 Gross Domestic Product of most countries in the world" (Baldé et al., 2018, p. 7).

Clearly, we need more rigorous enforcement of existing e-waste regulation, at national, regional, and global levels, and governmental policies and programs to stimulate the movement of recycling from the informal to formal sectors. Those policies should include mandatory extended producer responsibility, which requires companies like Samsung to ensure cradle-to-grave welfare for the devices that enrich them. Ragpickers must be encouraged to join the formal economy, provided with safe equipment for recycling, and trained in its use. This is an urgent matter of public health that can also generate economic benefits.

The multiple issues associated with e-waste present us with very compelling reasons to hold on to our phones for as long as possible. The waste stream is already filled with enough discarded digital devices to overwhelm the capacity of existing e-waste management systems. If we must replace our smartphones, let's wait until they are truly beyond repair. Then we should do our damnedest to make sure they get to a reputable and tested recycler or back to the original manufacturers.

So in terms of its carbon footprint, your smartphone is among the greenest electronic devices out there. It starts its life with a huge negative impact on the environment, punching above its weight in environmental harm relative to other devices, but makes up for this in low overall electricity consumption during its lifespan. And as more of us use cellphones to watch streamed content, we also make a dent in carbon emissions by reducing the sales and usage of higher-impact devices like TVs and PCs.

But we must never forget the workers making and disassembling our smartphones, and the pressure the industry exerts on them. Solidarity with them, and keeping your phone for as long as possible, make it as green as it can be. Don't let the powerful propaganda we outline in the next chapter fool you into thinking otherwise.

THREE

Calling Bullshit on Anti-Science Propaganda

So far, we've learned how to be smarter and more health-conscious about smartphones by understanding the risks of digital distractions and wireless radiation and appreciating the labor that both brings them to us as shiny new devices then relieves us of them when their technological sublimity has worn off. The precautionary principle serves as an excellent guide for both personal and social efforts to tame our attachment to these devices and mitigate exposure to potentially harmful electromagnetic and radiofrequency radiation. Some countries have enacted laws that strive for greater protection of cellphone users and their wireless environments.

We've also seen that there are three good environmental justifications for hanging onto the smartphones we already own. Doing so contributes less often to the problem of e-waste, a global disaster for ecosystems and the atmosphere; reduces carbon emissions, which are highest when new phones are manufactured and lowest over the smartphone's useful lifetime (compared to other digital devices); and de-pressurizes market demands that systematically pull millions of young people into intensive and hazardous factory conditions, where the length of the workday and the pace of production are dictated by brand companies and their annual promotions of dubious upgrades (not to mention their lack of responsibility for dealing with discarded products).

Along the way, we've encountered resistance to making our smartphones and wireless environment greener and safer. We saw that the CTIA is using US courts to fight attempts by cities to share and augment the FCC's tepid warnings about the possible carcinogenic effects of smartphones. CTIA spends millions of dollars each year convincing lawmakers that they run a safe and reasonable business. One result is that agencies like the FCC favor the very industries they were meant to regulate on our behalf, relinquishing their duty to protect us from known and potential risks. Among other things, this makes it more difficult to find scientific information about cellphone radiation, even the questionable SAR found in obscure legal notices that are posted in phones themselves. And we've seen how the vast majority of e-waste recycling operates in the shadows of illegality. The cellphone is a shady customer indeed, concealing the work that makes it and disposes of it, the impact it has on users, and the devastation it wreaks on miners, manufacturers, and recyclers.

Much of this hidden truth is the responsibility of propagandists for the industries involved, who operate ideologically as per the model of extractive capital. The fossil-fuel sector has been aware for decades that energy from coal and petrochemicals saturates the atmosphere with the greenhouse gases that are responsible for global warming. It has been involved in a vast, long-term propaganda campaign to deny this knowledge and cover up the extractive industries' role in the climate crisis (Hall, 2015).

Likewise, the telecommunications industry has long been aware of mobile-phone radiation risks from research on microwave radiation, which began during World War II (Cook et al., 1980). Studies conducted in the late 1970s on microwave (non-ionizing, or thermal) radiation in the US and the then Soviet Union corroborated harmful effects, including the disruption of biological development (learning ability and immunological systems), eye and brain deterioration, and possible genetic and birth defects (Massey, 1979, pp. 116–20). Electronics-industry researchers, many contracted to develop mobile technologies for the military, downplayed these effects and lobbied official standard-setting committees for the exclusion of

"The cellphone is a shady customer indeed."

cellular telephony from regulations being proposed in the late 1970s and through the 1980s (Kane, 2001, pp. 117–51).

The lobbying worked. US bodies responsible for determining safe exposure levels, the American National Standards Institute and the Institute of Electrical and Electronics Engineers, agreed to exempt cellphones from standards set for radiofrequency radiation in the 1980s. That gave the green light to developing the mobile-phone market, and further undercut the FCC's authority to impose safer exposure standards on cell-phones (Kane, 2001, p. 153).

This was not unprecedented. Since the late 1960s, the Commission had abdicated responsibility for monitoring health and safety hazards associated with telecommunications technologies, defining its primary role as serving the market by "ensuring an efficient, reliable and economic radio communications system" (Massey, 1979, p. 141). As one research scientist and cellphone design engineer pointed out: "If it were not for the categorical exclusion that exempted port-able cellular telephones from any radiation exposure regulations, the devices would have been barred from the marketplace as unsafe for humans" (Kane, 2001, p. 118).

We need to focus on the hundreds of millions

of dollars dedicated to anti-scientific propaganda and political lobbying (Funk and Rainie, 2015) and recognize these disinformation campaigns as a means for powerful political and economic interests to reject ideas and actions that would make smartphones and other electricity-dependent devices greener. We must learn when to call "bullshit."

Forewarned, Forearmed

There is enough research on how digital technologies affect biophysical environments to mitigate the worst features of planetary digital despoliation. But much scientific information is ignored or distorted by corporations, governments, and the media. There is a wide array of well-heeled philanthropic organizations that deny the truth and peddle climate-change misinformation (Farrell, 2019). Coin-operated intellectuals help polluting industries fend off pro-environmental legislation, "dissipate pressure for progress" (Miller and Dinan, 2015, p. 99), attack the character of environmentalists, and undermine the legitimacy of climate science.

Every day, reams of environmental news stories fail to make headlines in the mainstream press ("Top Environmental News," n.d.). The media are generally averse to technical scientific reports, especially when they provide ambiguous, ambivalent findings that require judicious, informed interpretation – caution, not revelation. Although most of us care that the planet is heating up and worry about our own contribution (Schwartz, 2019), journalists seem to believe we are uninterested in causal explanations of the phenomenon, especially technical ones. If a study asserts that the Earth's warming harms a flower's ability to produce sweet aromas, but scientific journalism shies away from technical discussions, we may not learn about the mechanism of "phenylpropanoid-based floral scent production" (the chemical basis of the plant's perfume) or its related impact on "plant-pollinator mutualism" (confused bees). Journalists act as if we want to avoid big words and scientific concepts, that we prefer a simple "yes or no" answer to global warming (Cna'ani et al., 2015).

Journalism increasingly looks for ways to compete with social media's annexation of audience curiosity. Many news organizations that are striving to survive in the digital economy reduce environmental reporting to such binary questions because they want to entice readers to click through articles and thereby add to the number of advertisements viewed each day (Frampton, 2015). We know that a wider contextual factor is the news media's transformation into profit centers rather than servants of the public interest, and their subsequent disinvestment in investigative reporting. Those changes have diminished public trust in journalism and disabled the informational media from responding to distortions in a consistently robust manner (Boykoff and Yulsman, 2013).

Broadcast radio and television networks veer between drastic reductions in coverage and narrating climate and environmental news within political, moral, and business frames (Seifter, Robbins, and Kalhoefer, 2016). And there is a disconnection between gee-whiz commercial-media coverage of smartphones as social phenomena and attention to global e-waste, which is largely neglected (Good, 2016). One study of mainstream media depictions of e-waste dumps in China and Ghana identified Western journalists attempting to create a sense of urgency over e-waste exports from the Global North to the Global South. Much like BAN's documentation of hazardous e-waste exports to Asia and Africa, these reports used a moral frame intended to create sympathy and dramatic engagement with a "site of suffering." But unlike BAN's reporting, they exhibited a certain detachment from ragpickers, giving the impression that their workplaces were "strange, almost alien spaces [of] sublime imagery." The effect of this "sublime strangeness" was to depict e-waste as "something that takes place 'over there' and not in our homes" (Andersson, 2017, p. 274) and to depict ragpickers as victims rather than subjects with some agency and the desire to protest and resist their conditions (Radulovic, 2018).

When it comes to health risks associated with cellphone radiation, the relevant science is never encapsulated in easy answers, as we saw in our examination of the NTP and Ramazzini Institute cancer studies in Chapter 1. Media coverage of the NTP draft report was largely equivocal and misleading, as the key clickbait headlines show: *The New York Times:* "Cancer Risk from Cellphone Radiation is Small, Studies Show"[1] (Grady, 2018); *Mother Jones*: "'Game-Changing' Study Links Cellphone Radiation to Cancer" (Harkinson, 2016); *The Wall Street Journal*: "US Cellphone Study Fans Cancer Concerns" (Knutson, 2016); *The Washington Post*: "Do Cellphones Cause Cancer? Don't Believe the Hype" (Feltman, 2016); and from *Vox*, the most clickable of all, "Seriously, Stop With the Irresponsible Reporting on Cellphones and Cancer" (Plumer, 2016).

---

[1] In 2016, the *New York Times* science reporter, Gina Kolata, narrated a video telling people that it's absolutely fine to use cellphones (Laffen and Kolata, 2016).

Most of the headlines leave the impression there is no clear answer or way to find the truth. We might as well be listening to 1940s radio serials funded by commercials extolling the safety of smoking by quoting doctors on the value of particular brands for ensuring healthy throats.[2]

Studies of the environment are frequently complicated, ongoing, and not given to pronouncements of absolute certainty, except on the broad issue of human-caused climate change. This has made coverage of global warming and radiation risks from electronics vulnerable to misinterpretation when reporters employ the 'he said/she said' model of investigation, which leaves readers wondering where the truth lies. This mythical two-sides-to-every-story magic pervades and degrades US journalism schools and newsrooms. Even today, after scientists have reached consensus on the human causes of global warming, unthinking journalistic practices give license to naysayers and the lingering doubts they peddle in the name of objectivity: the mainstream US press frequently allocates equal time to different perspectives on climate change, however unscientific their

[2] Though nothing can compete with Lucky Strike's simple promise of "never a rough puff." (http://www.oldtimeradiofans.com/ old_radio_commercials/Lucky_Strike_Cigarettes.mp3).

claims may be (Hart and Feldman, 2014; Maxwell and Miller, 2016). This has become a particular problem because right-wing political parties anxious to distance themselves from expertise, science, and professionalism, and ready to point to press coverage inimical to those goals as biased against them, use climate-change denial as a litmus test (Bolsen and Shapiro, 2018).

We are also exposed to contrarian claims boosted by a largely unregulated public-relations industry. It works assiduously to cultivate science deniers as legitimate, worthy of respect, and deserving of media coverage. In addition to the traditional news media, scientific evidence for the costs of climate change has also been obscured by new communications companies. They use Facebook, Twitter, YouTube, and Google, *inter alia*, to spread misleading ideas among ideologues, demagogues, journalists, politicians, and members of the public (Sunstein, 2017; Taplin, 2017; Sumpter, 2018).

The propaganda is so powerful that even some experts, bombarded by nonsense and charlatanism, react in ways that give some slack to the refuted arguments of contrarians. Scientists often take the bait when a contrarian idea is dangled before them, but downplay the severity of global warming in the name of calm reflection. And their confidence can be rattled by public stereotyping, the bashing of their profession, or outright smear tactics that label them "alarmists," "arrogant," or "cowards" (a charge made when they avoid debate with bloviating deniers). When contrarian views are depicted as majority opinions on Fox News and other anti-science media, laypeople and scientists alike may react by thinking their concerns about global warming are not shared by most of the population, or even their colleagues. This mass-mediated pressure can make the staunchest advocate of climate science doubt themselves publicly, running the risk of tacitly admitting that climate change is controversial (Lewandowsky et al., 2015).

Just describing something as controversial is a powerful propaganda technique of its own (Maxwell and Miller, 2016). Although it suppresses the fact that there is no controversy about human-caused climate change within the scientific community, the uncertainty promoted is alluring. It triggers what economists call "ambiguity aversion," which favors inaction and condones business as usual by urging us to stick with the devil we know, even if that dooms us to eternal suffering (Lewandowsky et al., 2015, p. 2). Disagreements among climate experts appearing in the media tend to be perceived as evidence of the underlying science's weakness. For while skepticism is a research scientist's stock-in-trade, it can play negatively with journalists and non-specialist publics who are averse to ambiguity. The propaganda that ensues from unethical coverage of uncertainty is dominated by conservatives, aghast at the prospect of a scientifically driven, democratic regulation of industries (Tranter, 2017).

Some climate scientists have challenged the denialist propaganda head on, reasserting the importance of science's "self-correcting" machinery and the critical checks of "peer review and professional challenges" that provide the "good faith skepticism" that questions "every minute detail" of new research to hold scientists to high standards of independent inquiry. Climate scientist Michael Mann and cartoonist Tom Toles provide compelling and humorous examples of how to thwart denialists, whose arguments "dodge evidence" they don't like while spinning fact-free contrarianism. Mann takes on the denialists who have attacked his famous research that showed a spike in warming in the late nineteenth century after a thousand years of relatively minor variations in temperature changes – better known as the hockey-stick curve (2016). Search for "Michael Mann" and "hockey stick" and you'll see that assaults on his work and reputation continue apace.

Researchers of cellphone radiation, by contrast, run up against other scientists' faith in, as well as media misinformation about, the null hypothesis that says non-ionizing radiation from mobile phones should not cause cancer. In this case, there really is dissensus. As we saw in Chapter 1, the big news surrounding the NTP and Ramazzini Institute studies was their refutation of the null hypothesis. But most reporting buried what should have led the coverage, blundering instead into their comfort zone: the ambiguity of supposed balance. In effect, the media suppressed key research on radiofrequency radiation and cancer risks. The watchdog Project Censored ranked scientific findings of causal links between cellphone radiation and cancer the fourth most important censored news story of 2017–18 (2018).

War-Gaming Science

Unsurprisingly, most research that finds few or no negative health effects from smartphones tends to be corporate-financed. Hired "skeptics" work to muddy public thinking with the claim that there are two sides to every story. This might fit the aforementioned, dodgy journalistic routines of balance, but it is unsuitable when the health of mobile users is at stake. The war-gaming of science – attacking evidence of harm – worked well for the tobacco corporations for many years, until industry hacks and the hacking coughers they cultivated could no longer deny that these products caused sickness and death (Davis, 2010). Many of the same "merchants of doubt" who contest climate science perfected their swindle selling those lies in the 1960s (Oreskes and Conway, 2010). Consider the mendacity of this tobacco executive, who said in a 1969 internal memo:

> Doubt is our product since it is the best means of competing with the "body of fact" that exists in the mind of the general public. It is also the means of establishing a controversy. Within the business we recognize that a controversy exists. However, with the general public the consensus is that cigarettes are in some way harmful to the health. If we are successful in establishing a controversy at the public level, then there is an opportunity to put across the real facts about smoking and health. Doubt is also the limit of our "product." (quoted in Readfearn, 2015)

The tobacco industry continues to employ "more than 100 free-market thinktanks from North America to Europe and south Asia" to help sell its poisons, war-game science, and raise money (Glenza, 2019).

Graham Readfearn has detailed the "four main cogs

"Hired 'skeptics' work to muddy public thinking with the claim that there are two sides to every story."

that make up the machinery" of the doubt business: "conservative 'free market' thinktanks, public relations groups, fossil fuel organizations, and ideologically aligned media" (2015). Sifting through internal documents from the fossil fuel industry, he identifies lobbyists, thinktanks, and PR professionals that have conspired with the industry for decades on misinformation campaigns about climate change. Readfearn quotes a notorious 2000 memo that US Republican consultant Frank Luntz produced to guide the energy industry's propaganda:

> Should the public come to believe that the scientific issues are settled, their views about global warming will change accordingly. Therefore, you need to continue to make the lack of scientific certainty a primary issue in the debate. (Luntz, 2000)

Luntz modified this advice in 2003 in a "language advisory" he wrote for the George W. Bush administration called "Winning the Global Warming Debate: An Overview." Luntz urged the White House to replace the phrase "global warming" with "climate change" because, he said, climate change is "less frightening" and its passive construction conveys a sense that no one is to blame (quoted in Lakoff, 2010, p. 71).

There are some positive developments. The whistle

was well-and-truly blown on climate-change denying, coin-operated intellectuals in 2019 when Shell broke ranks with industry norms and dissociated itself from associations dedicated to deceitful conduct about climate change. It did so in the nicest, most polite way. But the die was cast (Royal Dutch Shell, 2019). And the Italian Supreme Court has challenged the mobile industry's war-gaming tactic. In 2012, it ordered authorities to pay workers' compensation to a former businessman who developed a tumor in his head because of heavy, long-term use of a cellphone. The court threw out industry-funded studies presented as "evidence," on the grounds that they were tainted by conflict of interest. It accepted independent research that suggested a causal link between cellphone use and cancer (Alimenti, 2012; International Commission for Electromagnetic Safety, 2012).

Shareholder Activism

Shareholder activism has changed since the Securities and Exchange Commission added the Shareholder Proposal Rule to the Securities Exchange Act of 1934, allowing US shareholders (stockholders) to submit proposals to alter company operations (Mueller, 1998).

For the first thirty years of such activism, proposals targeted growth and profits, largely because the Federal government did not require companies to inform shareholders, via proxy statements, about "social issue" resolutions that were submitted to management.

A legal decision in 1970 made it possible for shareholders to vote on proposals to modify corporate policy in ways that could have important social outcomes, such as reducing environmental harm or expanding workers' rights. This opened the door for individual and institutional investors, foundations, charities, and religious and other organizations to file issue-oriented shareholder resolutions. Market fundamentalists have been fighting back ever since (Goranova and Ryan, 2014).

Contrarians seek to sow doubt among shareholders about corporate leaders who promote green practices within their companies, which they denounce as anathematic to free-market principles. The National Center for Public Policy Research (NCPPR), a conservative thinktank, issued a shareholder resolution to Apple in 2014, demanding information on the company's "associations and memberships and trade associations that work on [environmental] sustainability issues," ostensibly to help other shareholders see how Apple had come under the ideological influence of anti-market forces.

NCPPR lost the vote, but claimed victory for the stunt, which it hoped would cast doubt on the credibility of Apple's top managers (Makower, 2014). The business press would probably have ignored the event were it not for Cook's reaction to this market fundamentalism. He shot back: "I don't consider the bloody ROI [return on investment]" when designing devices for the blind, environmental betterment, or worker safety. "If you want me to do things only for ROI reasons," he said, "you should get out of this stock" (quoted in Russell, 2014). The likes of NCPPR represent capitalist chorines who are "tired of supporting corporations that support the left." A central tenet of the group is that "private owners are the best stewards of the environment." Zombie market fundamentalists and their op-ed bleating, "report"-writing thinktanks love this BS.

Shareholder activism, even more than consumer activism, is fundamentally plutocratic – the wealthiest get the most votes. The strategy of contrarian operatives like NCPPR is to infect the shareholder agenda with anti-environmental discourse. They use old canards that greening industry will kill jobs, diminish the value of stocks, and shake faith in free markets. They sometimes win, but activists with a social agenda often prove more skillful at nudging management to act.

In 2018, two of Apple's largest shareholders – Jana

Partners and the California State Teachers' Retirement System – who controlled about two billion dollars of Apple stock, beseeched the company leadership to help young people fight cellphone addiction (Gibbs, 2018). In Chapter 1, we mentioned the regret that many Silicon Valley moguls have expressed for creating addictive technologies. So it is unsurprising that Apple responded favorably, adding a feature to its iOS 12 operating system called Screen Time to help consumers manage the time they spent on their phones by setting limits on access to social media and other content (Nicas, Chen, and Manjoo, 2018). Good for Apple. But as we'll see in the Conclusion, a similar feature was already available in another smartphone, the greenest aspirant on the market – the Fairphone.

It's hard to transcend the weapons of misinformation wielded by rich and powerful electronics corporations, fossil-fuel industrialists, telecommunications firms, and their craven/gullible supporters. They have built a vast doubt industry that bombards us with propaganda so they can keep polluting the environment, heating up the atmosphere, and preventing a greener future. Despite the challenges we face, we can win by knowing how and when to call bullshit on them and their media allies. That means engaging in activism over climate change and requiring governments to legislate safeguards of the truth – so that *any* time coin-operated shill appears on our screens, so should researchers capable of providing us with the latest findings.

What Next?

End Dependence

It's time to pierce the mists of digital enchantment that are pumped into our media environment by cellphone companies, telecommunications lobbyists, and their fellow propagandists. We must wake up to digital ecological damage and our role in it, and heed calls from the green youth movement to act now and discredit attempts to fool us. We know how to reduce the massive levels of conventional pollution. We may not stop the sixth great extinction, but we might conserve certain habitats and mitigate our rapidly diminishing biodiversity.

Cellphones are one way of communicating with one another and developing solidarity over such social change – but they are also part of the problem. Telecommunications firms have built an inefficient infrastructure that cannot be easily or cheaply replaced. And infrastructural and service policies have been rigged to relieve corporations of public-interest obligations to make telephony green and affordable. Telecommunications multinationals understand that this level of energy consumption is a threat to both the environment and their continuing market domination. Their corporate response has so far focused on technical fixes, with some deceptively playful interactive tools,[1] but little concern for the wider public interest. These companies concentrate on raising demand, working against environmental regulation, and keeping their place in the growing market for green-branded, "smart" technologies.[2]

We can limit their hegemony by slowing the pace of product turnover that fills retailers' shelves and website advertisements with a continual array of new smartphones. We can call a halt to saturating the waste stream with seemingly outdated, unwanted rejects, insisting on a pause in order to eradicate the atrocious conditions of cellphone workers around the world. We can rein in the promoters of 5G networks, cease the unthinking deployment of this newest example of "technological progress," and require independent scientific analysis

[1] http://gwatt.net/

[2] http://www.verizon.com/about/news/ge-and-verizon-take-energy-efficiency-and-sustainability/

of health risks before accepting ever-greater radiofrequency radiation.

If we don't end our dependence on the symbolic value of new, shiny smartphones, the odds are against us and our representative governments and institutions slapping much-needed rules on the mendacious telecommunications industry. We need policies that make the full range of cultural, informational, and educational resources available to everyone, not just those who can afford them. There will always be a place for the joys of shopping – but alternative, low-wattage joys should be more ubiquitous than mobile cellular networks.

Break the Bonds of the Supply Chain: The Idea of the Fairphone

The 2013 plan for the Fairphone, a Dutch invention, was to avoid the worst aspects of the global supply chain – conflict minerals, hazardous working conditions, and carbon emissions – from mines to e-waste salvage yards and every workplace in between – while still providing features that we love. For consumers trying to limit their carbon footprint, Fairphone has some clear advantages, such as modular components that owners can remove for repair or replacement, thereby lengthening the life of the phone (Harris, 2018).[3] Fairphones are still energy-intensive at birth, but much greener than the norm thereafter. Designed for green smartphone users who show regard for the workers who make their devices, the company's future success will depend not only on that market but on persuading governmental, military, bureaucratic, educational, and corporate entities to come on board.

Fairphone has demonstrated to other brands that an alternative supply chain is possible (The Dragonfly Initiative and Fairphone, 2017). The founders discovered that you can't do this from scratch; you have to go to the existing industry and try to change it. The biggest hurdle they face is their minuscule market position – they have simply not been influential in redesigning the supply chain. This is typical of small-scale attempts at sustainable environmental governance that lack structural market and oligarchic power, relying instead on "dialogue, persuasion and coalition-building" (Biefendorf et al., 2019).

Despite its limited market power, Fairphone has made a difference to workers' lives along the supply

---

[3] Google tried to make a modular phone (the Ara) but scrapped the project in 2016 for reasons of cost. Its prototypes ended up in a basic form with non-modular, non-upgradable parts (Statt, 2016).

chain (Jindra et al., 2019). Imagine if other brands took its aspiration for an ethical design seriously and used their suppliers. Had Google adopted the Fairphone production model for the Pixel phone, for example, the firm's scale and market power might have enhanced a greener supply chain's attractiveness and made ethical design a competitive option for manufacturers and other brands.

Ethical design aimed at protecting consumers from the potentially harmful effects of phones, from radiation to mental distraction and other ills, is also important. And while we welcome Screen Time as part of iPhone software, we should point out that Fairphone has had a similar feature, called "peace of mind," for years. More importantly, Fairphone has called upon the movement for ethical design to do more than make consumer experiences healthier. It has appealed to institutional and individual consumers dedicated to de-growth and a green economy (Haucke, 2018).

Fairphone's idea of redesigning the entire smartphone supply chain from start to finish requires dominant telecommunications and electronics corporations to get on board. Ask your political representatives, ask the maker of your favorite phone, ask young engineers designing a new generation of cellular mobile devices: Why can't our phones be more like a Fairphone? If

"Why can't our phones be more like a Fairphone?"

they answer that the supply chain won't let us, you can call BS.

Imbue Supply Chains with Compassion – 164 Years Later

In 1855, Herman Melville – disillusioned by the flop of *Moby-Dick; or the Whale* four years earlier – published a short story in *Harper's New Monthly Magazine* entitled "The Paradise of Bachelors and the Tartarus of Maids." The first part recounts an American narrator's visit to London "in the smiling month of May." He meets a group of well-heeled bachelor lawyers, and they share kingly amounts of food, drink, and travelers' tales. The second part finds the narrator traveling in a mid-winter snowstorm to an isolated New England paper mill, where he hopes to secure mailing envelopes for his lucrative seed business (Melville, 1855).

In stark juxtaposition to the paradise of bachelors, he observes female millworkers confined to a hellish repetition of rag preparation, pulping, pressing, and folding – their faces "pale with work, and blue with cold"; their eyes "supernatural with unrelated misery." The mill owner tells him that they are all unmarried – the "maids" of the title – because married women are "apt to be off-and-on too much. We want none but steady workers: twelve hours to the day, day after day, through three hundred sixty-five days."

The bachelors and maids live worlds apart, divided by stratifications of geography, wealth, class, and gender as well as experiences of time, space, and risk. The bachelor gentlemen of leisure measure the hours by "a wine chronometer," with each pour a counterpoint to conviviality. Conversely, for the women workers, the "metallic necessity, the unbudging fatality" of the clock at the mill's heart sets workflow to an "unvarying punctuality and precision."

The bachelors perceive an expansive world from their perch at the center of the British Empire. The same imperium isolates women in the periphery, restricting them from a life beyond the underworld prison of the assembly line, the Tartarus of maids. The men's fine apparel and good health contrast with the dangerous and toxic conditions of the mill, especially in the rag room, where the workers drag strips of cloth across the blades of a "glittering scythe… thus ripping asunder every seam, and converting the tatters almost into lint." The girls "don't cough," even though the "air swam with the fine, poisonous particles, which from all sides darted, subtilely, as motes in sun-beams, into the lungs." The narrator can barely breathe.

Melville was writing at a time when recycled cotton and linen rags were primary raw materials for industrial papermaking, years before innovations in chemical processing made wood fiber a viable resource. Insightfully, he connects the dots between the millworkers and socially marginal ragpickers in London who collected clothing from rubbish to sell for export to the US, where cloth for the mills was in short supply through most of the nineteenth century (Maxwell and Miller, 2012). "'Tis not unlikely, then," says Melville's narrator, "that among these heaps of rags there may be some old shirts, gathered from the dormitories of the Paradise of Bachelors."

These two distant groups were bound to each other through a global economy that tied the cosmopolitan fortunes of elites to the factory misfortunes of workers at the outer edges of the capitalist system – a story of technological labor that has remained largely unchanged since the age of print. Even today, workers in the periphery rarely appear in accounts of high-tech's provenance – new technologies all seem to flow from geniuses at Apple, Google, Microsoft, and their kind, who form an aristocracy of talent living in conditions uncannily akin to Melville's paradise of bachelors. DRC workers excavating minerals with their bare hands, PRC women wasting away in factories day and night, and Mexican ragpickers recycling e-waste perilously just do not make as good a story as a narrative focused on febrile figures sitting around in shirtsleeves in Northern California waiting for a muse to alight on their shoulders and inspire them.

We saw in the Introduction that the labor process and environment are beyond the ken of "visionaries" at the Mobile World Congress, who were advised to "move beyond technology evangelism and start working toward crafting innovative business-driven solutions that address real-world issues" (ABI Research for Visionaries/MWC 19 Barcelona, 2019).

As Melville sensed in his day, we must tell stories that make the labor process visible. Would he be surprised to learn that today's workforce in electronics factories in Mexico, China, and elsewhere is still mostly young, unmarried women? There's not been much gender progress in the new paradise of digital bachelors either – roughly speaking, he would have to substitute a woman for one of the nine lawyers in his story to reflect the small number of women working at Silicon Valley's electronics boys' clubs, where conditions can be disheartening, alienating, and in some cases, as in "Gamergate," life-threatening (Miller, 2014; Wu, 2015). One of America's most renowned novelists connected dots that were separated by distance and inequality, and he did so in the nineteenth century. We can do the same for today.

To change the supply chain, we must see the world with Melville's acuity and compassion. There are already organizations built on just such combinations. Consider Guadalajara's Centro de Reflexión y Acción Laboral/ Center for Labor Reflection and Action; Weltwirtschaft, Ökologie and Entwicklung/World Economy, Ecology and Development's Buy IT Fair campaign in Berlin;[4] Students and Scholars Against Corporate Misbehavior/ 大學師生監察無良企業行動,[5] based in Hong Kong; Women in Informal Employment: Globalizing and Organizing[6] from Manchester; the Good Electronics Network of Amsterdam;[7] Amnesty's reporting;[8] China Labor Watch/中国劳工观察 in Gotham;[9] and Seattle's Basel Action Network.[10] The Global Alliance of Waste Pickers[11] represents those who must deal with the detritus of abandoned electronics. There is an International Campaign for Responsible Technology based in

[4] https://www.weed-online.org/themen/english.html

[5] http://sacom.hk/zh/

[6] http://www.wiego.org/

[7] https://goodelectronics.org/

[8] https://www.amnesty.org/en/documents/afr62/3183/2016/en/

[9] http://chinalaborwatch.org/home.aspx

[10] https://www.ban.org/

[11] https://globalrec.org/es/

Colombia,[12] and an Electronics Take Back Coalition.[13] Follow them, befriend them, donate to them, learn from them, and contribute to acuity and compassion along the supply chain. The price of your smartphone is much greater than the purchase and subscriptions costs that will appear on your debit card.

Optimism of the Intelligence, Optimism of the Will

There is much in the current state of global affairs to dismay and dishearten. But pessimism and cynicism are not good starting points for a green agenda (Suzuki and Dressel, 2002). We can halt our disastrous impact on the Earth and its atmosphere, and push for greener designs of our devices and a humane supply chain to bring them to us.

A century ago, the French Nobel laureate Romain Rolland called for "pessimism of the intelligence, which penetrates every illusion, and optimism of the will" (quoted in Fisher, 1988). That remarkable blend of thinking realistically in search of utopian goals is crucial.

[12] http://www.icrt.co/
[13] http://www.electronicstakeback.com/

The sociologist Erik Olin Wright taught us to keep utopia alive and despair on the margins. He called for optimism of the intelligence as well as the will, recognizing that the struggle to "create real utopias" necessitated "showing that another world is possible by building it in the spaces available, and then pushing against the state and public policy to expand those spaces" (2012: 22).

In environmental terms, that means facing *up* to the facts, not the distortions, of climate change and human pollution; facing *down* mendacious and gullible naysayers; insisting on realistic science education; denouncing supine media coverage that bows before the false idol of capital; and calling for renewed, revitalized laws, regulations, and enforcement by governments in keeping with international standards.

A smartphone might not seem like a starting point for emancipatory politics. But the little device you're holding in your hand (at a safe distance from your body) is connected to a bigger world in need of help. Let it be a reminder that we have the ingenuity to make our devices greener – and the world, too.

"By the Numbers: How Long Will Your Appliances Last? It Depends" (2009, March 21) *Consumer Reports News* https://www.consumer reports.org/cro/news/2009/03/by-the-numbers-how-long-will-your -appliances-last-it-depends/index.htm.

"Children's Climate Rallies Gain Momentum in Europe" (2019, January 25) *BBC News* https://www.bbc.co.uk/news/world-europe-46999381.

"Chinese City Moves Electronics Recycling Activities to Industrial Park" (2015, December 18) *Recycling Today* http://www.recycling today.com/article/ban-guiyu-industrial-park-visit/.

Conflicted: The Fight Over Congo's Minerals (2019, March 3) *Al Jazeera* https://www.aljazeera.com/programmes/faultlines/2015/11/conflic ted-fight-congo-minerals-151118084541495.html.

Conflict Minerals, Rebels and Child Soldiers in Congo (2012, May 22) *Vice* https://www.youtube.com/watch?v=kYqrflGpTRE.

Congo: Blood, Gold and Mobile Phones (2011, September 6) *Guardian* https://www.youtube.com/watch?v=gGuG0Ios8ZA.

Electronic Waste in Ghana (2008, August 4) Greenpeace International https://www.youtube.com/watch?v=pr1zQrXM_7s.

"In Guiyu, the E-Waste Nightmare is Far From Over" (2016, November 4) *Toxic Leaks* https://toxicleaks.com/wiki/In_Guiyu,_ the_e-waste_nightmare_is_far_from_over.

Made in China: Mobile Phone Factory Behind the Scenes (2017, November 28) *BBC News* https://www.youtube.com/watch?v= hwMZtdTcM7A.

References

"The Maturing of the Smartphone Industry is Cause for Celebration" (2019, January 10) *The Economist* https://www.economist.com/leaders/2019/01/12/the-maturing-of-the-smartphone-industry-is-cause-for-celebration.

"Political Will to Fight Climate Change is Fading, Warns UN Chief" (2019, May 12) *BBC News* https://www.bbc.com/news/av/world-asia-48244315/political-will-to-fight-climate-change-is-fading-warns-un-chief.

"Progress and Challenges of Conflict Minerals" (2018) *The Enough Project* https://enoughproject.org/wp-content/uploads/Progress-and-challenges-June-2018.pdf.

The Secret Inside Your Cellphone (2017, March 24) Canadian Broadcasting Corporation *CBC Marketplace* https://www.youtube.com/watch?v=Wm69ik_Qdb8&feature=youtu.be.

Special Report: Inside the Congo Cobalt Mines That Exploit Children (2017, February 27) *Sky News* https://www.youtube.com/watch?v=JcJ8me22NVs.

"Top Environmental News" (n.d.) *Science Daily* https://www.sciencedaily.com/news/top/environment/.

ToxiCity: Life at Agbobloshie, the World's Largest E-Waste Dump in Ghana (2016, June 1) *RT* https://www.youtube.com/watch?v=mleQVO1Vd1I.

5G Appeal (2017, September 13) "Scientists Warn of Potential Serious Health Effects of 5G," Environmental Health Trust https://ehtrust.org/wp-content/uploads/Scientist-5G-appeal-2017.pdf. ABI Research for Visionaries/MWC 19 Barcelona (2019) *The Future of the Mobile Industry: A Reality Check from Mobile World Congress 2019 – 6 Brief Reads for Visionaries* https://go.abiresearch.com/2019-mobile-world-congress-reality-check.

Agence Nationale des Fréquences (n.d.) DAS Téléphonie Mobile https://data.anfr.fr.

References

Aguayo, A. (2015, June 24) "Yonquis del Móvil," *El País* https://elpais.com/elpais/2015/06/23/estilo/1435080230_473059.html.

Agur, C. (2015) "Second-Order Networks, Gambling, and Corruption on Indian Mobile Phone Networks," *Media, Culture and Society*, 37, no. 5: 768–83.

Aitkenhead, D. (2019, May 3) "Madonna on Motherhood and Fighting Ageism," *Vogue* https://www.vogue.co.uk/article/madonna-on-ageing-and-motherhood.

Alimenti, V. (2012, October 19) "Italy Court Ruling Links Mobile Phone Use to Tumor," *Reuters* https://www.reuters.com/article/us-italy-phones/italy-court-ruling-links-mobile-phone-use-to-tumor-idUSBRE89I0V320121019.

Alster, N. (2015) *Captured Agency: How the Federal Communications Commission Is Dominated by the Industries It Presumably Regulates*. Edmond J. Safra Center for Ethics http://ethics.harvard.edu/files/center-for-ethics/files/capturedagency_alster.pdf.

Álvarez, M. Á. P. (2014, May) "Latin America"s Digital Divide," *Latin American Science* http://latinamericanscience.org/2014/05/latin-americas-digital-divide/.

American Academy of Pediatrics (2013, August 29) "Letter to Acting Chairwoman Clyburn (FCC) and Commissioner Hamburg (FDA)" https://ecfsapi.fcc.gov/file/7520941318.pdf.

American Cancer Institute (2018, November) "Cellular Phones" https://www.cancer.org/cancer/cancer-causes/radiation-exposure/cellular-phones.html.

Anderson, C. and Wolff, M. (2010, August 17) "The Web is Dead: Long Live the Internet," *Wired* http://www.wired.com/magazine/2010/08/ff_webrip/all/1.

Anderson, M. and Kumar, M. (2019) *Digital Divide Persists Even as Lower-Income Americans Make Gains in Tech Adoption*, Pew Research Center https://www.pewresearch.org/fact-tank/2019/05/07/digit

al-divide-persists-even-as-lower-income-americans-make-gains-in-tech-adoption/.

Andersson, L. (2017) "Where Technology Goes to Die: Representations of Electronic Waste in Global Television News," *Environmental Communication*, 11, no. 2: 263–75.

Aswani, S. (2016, May 31) "Leveraging Co-Location for Competitive Advantage in HFT," *HPC Wire* https://www.hpcwire.com/solution_content/hpe/financial-services/leveraging-co-location-competitive-advantage-hft/.

Atkinson, L. (2013) "Smart Shoppers? Using QR Codes and 'Green' Smartphone Apps to Mobilize Sustainable Consumption in the Retail Environment," *International Journal of Consumer Studies*, 37, no. 4: 387–93.

Baldé, C. P., Forti V., Gray, V., Kuehr, R., and Stegmann, P. (2018) *The Global E-Waste Monitor 2017*. Bonn/Geneva/Vienna: United Nations University, International Telecommunication Union, and International Solid Waste Association.

Basel Action Network (2016) "Scam Recycling: E-Dumping on Asia by US Recyclers" https://www.resource-recycling.com/images/BANReportTwo.pdf.

Basel Convention (1989) *Convention on the Control of Transboundary Movements of Hazardous Wastes and Their Disposal* http://www.basel.int/TheConvention/Overview/TextoftheConvention/tabid/1275/Default.aspx.

Beck, U. (2002) "The Cosmopolitan Society," *Theory, Culture and Society*, 19, nos. 1–2: 17–44.

Belkhir, L. and Elmeligi, A. (2018) "Assessing ICT Global Emissions Footprint: Trends to 2040," *Journal of Cleaner Production*, 177: 448–63.

Beren, S. (2018) "'Look Up': The Cell Phone Manifesto," *Media Theory*, 2, no. 2: 332–43.

References

Betteridge D. J. (2000) "What is Oxidative Stress?," *Metabolism*, 49, no. 2: 3–8.

Beurteaux, D. (2018, April 9) "Is Plastic Waste Poisoning Our Seafood?," *Pacific Standard* https://psmag.com/environment/is-plastic-poisoning-our-oci.

Bhandari, A. (2019) "Gender Inequality in Mobile Technology Access: The Role of Economic and Social Development," *Information, Communication and Society*, 22, no. 5: 678–94.

Bianchi, M. (2015, June 24) "Digital Age Inequality in Latin America," *democraciaAbierta* https://www.opendemocracy.net/democraciaabierta/mat%C3%ADas-bianchi/digital-age-inequality-in-latin-america.

Biefendorf, K., Van Eynde, S., and Bachus, K. (2019) "Environmental, Climate and Social Leadership of Small Enterprises: Fairphone's Step-by-Step Approach," *Environmental Politics*, 28, no. 1: 43–63.

Blincoe, L. J., Miller, T. R., Zaloshnja, E., and Lawrence, B. A. (2015) *The Economic and Societal Impact of Motor Vehicle Crashes, 2010, (Revised)* (Report No. DOT HS 8 12 013) National Highway Traffic Safety Administration https://crashstats.nhtsa.dot.gov/Api/Public/ViewPublication/812013.

Bolsen, T. and Shapiro, M. A. (2018) "The US News Media, Polarization on Climate Change, and Pathways to Effective Communication," *Environmental Communication*, 12, no. 2: 149–63.

Bowles, N. (2018, October 26) "A Dark Consensus About Screens and Kids Begins to Emerge in Silicon Valley," *The New York Times* https://www.nytimes.com/2018/10/26/style/phones-children-silicon-valley.html.

Boykoff, M. and Yulsman, Y. (2013) "Political Economy, Media, and Climate Change: Sinews of Modern Life," *WIREs Climate Change* http://sciencepolicy.colorado.edu/admin/publication_files/2013.19.pdf.

References

Bragazzi, N. L. and Del Puente, G. (2014) "A Proposal for Including Nomophobia in the New DSM-V," *Psychology Research and Behavior Management*, 7: 155–60.

Brecht, B. (1935) "Questions From a Worker Who Reads," *Marxists. org* https://www.marxists.org/subject/art/literature/brecht/.

Buyya, R. and Srirama, S. N., eds. (2019) *Fog and Edge Computing: Principles and Paradigms*. Hoboken: Wiley.

Callaway, A. (2017) *Demand the Supply*, The Enough Project https://enoughproject.org/wp-content/uploads/2017/11/DemandTheSupply_EnoughProject_2017Rankings_final.pdf.

Canadians for Safe Technology (n.d.) "5G on the Way – What is it and How Will it Affect Canadians' Health?," http://c4st.org/5g-coming-soon/.

The Carbon Trust (n.d.) *Carbon Bootprint of the FA Community Shield* https://www.carbontrust.com/media/360767/carbon-bootprint-infographic.pdf.

The Carbon Trust (2016) *The "Carbon Bootprint" of Euro 2016: Which Nation's Fans Have the Lowest Carbon Footprint When Watching Games* https://www.carbontrust.com/news/2016/06/the-carbon-bootprint-of-euro-2016-which-nations-fans-have-the-lowest-carbon-footprint-when-watching-games/.

Carlberg, M., Hedendahl, L., Koppel, T. and Hardell, L. (2019) "High Ambient Radiofrequency Radiation in Stockholm City, Sweden," *Oncology Letters*, 17, no. 2: 1777–83.

Castells, M., Fernández-Ardèvol, M., Linchuan Qiu, J., and Sey, A. (2007) *Mobile Communication and Society: A Global Perspective*. Cambridge, Mass.: MIT Press.

Catholic Agency for Overseas Development (2004) *Clean Up Your Computer: Working Conditions in the Electronics Sector* https://www.peacelink.it/cybercultura/docs/176.pdf.

Center for Responsive Politics (2018) *CTIA Open Secrets* https://

www.opensecrets.org/lobby/clientsum.php?id=D000000394& year=2018.

Centre for Energy-Efficient Telecommunications, Bell Labs, and University of Melbourne (2013, June) *The Power of Wireless Cloud: An Analysis of the Impact on Energy Consumption of the Growing Popularity of Accessing Cloud Services Via Wireless Services* http://www.ceet.unimelb.edu.au/publications/downloads/ceet-white-paper-wireless-cloud.pdf.

Chan, J. and Ho, C. (2008) *The Dark Side of Cyberspace: Inside the Sweatshops of China's Computer Hardware Production*. Berlin: World Economy, Ecology and Development.

Chan, J., Pun, N., and Selden, M. (2016) "Chinese Labor Protest and Trade Unions," in Maxwell, R., (ed.) *The Routledge Companion to Labor and Media*. New York: Routledge, pp. 290–302.

Chandel, S., Kaur, S. Issa, M., Singh, H. P., Batish, D. R., and Kohli, R. K. (2019) "Exposure to Mobile Phone Radiations at 2350 MHz Incites Cyto- and Genotoxic Effects in Root Meristems of *Allium Cepa*," *Journal of Environmental Health Science and Engineering* https://doi.org/10.1007/s40201-018-00330-1.

Chang, L. (2016, July 20) "Sex or Your Smartphone? Americans' Answers May Surprise You," *Digital Trends* https://www.digitaltrends.com/mobile/smartphone-addiction-2/.

Climate Group (2008) *Smart2020: Enabling the Low Carbon Economy in the Information Age*. London: Global Sustainability Initiative.

Cna'ani, A., Mühlemann, J. K., Ravid, J., Masci, T., Klempien, A., Nguyen, T. T. H., Dudareva, N., Pichersky, E., and Vainstein, A. (2015) "Petunia × Hybridafloral Scent Production is Negatively Affected by High-Temperature Growth Conditions," *Plant, Cell and Environment*, 38, no. 7: 1333–46.

Cohen, R. (2018, July 19) "Do Cellphones Cause Cancer? Government Study Reveals 'Stunningly Important' Findings," *Newsweek* https://

References

www.newsweek.com/2018/07/27/cancer-cellphones-ntp-findings-toxicologists-brain-cancer-us-1024633.html.

Cook, H. J., Steneck, N. H., Vander, A. J., and Kane, G. L. (1980) "Early Research on the Biological Effects of Microwave Radiation: 1940–1960," *Annals of Science*, 7: 323–51.

Crowston, B. (2018) "Smartphones: Behind the Screen," *Resonance,* 8: 9–10.

David, P., Kim, J-H., Brickman, J. S., Ran, W., and Curtis, C. M. (2015) "Mobile Phone Distraction While Studying," *New Media and Society*, 17, no. 10: 1661–79.

Davis, D. (2010) *Disconnect: The Truth About Cell Phone Radiation, What the Industry Has Done to Hide It, and How to Protect Your Family.* Boston: Dutton/Penguin.

Deloitte (2017) *Communications Infrastructure Upgrade: The Need for Deep Fiber* https://www2.deloitte.com/content/dam/Deloitte/us/Documents/technology-media-telecommunications/us-tmt-5GReady-the-need-for-deep-fiber-pov.pdf.

Deloitte (2018) *Global Mobile Consumer Survey, US Edition* https://www2.deloitte.com/content/dam/Deloitte/us/Documents/technology-media-telecommunications/us-tmt-global-mobile-consumer-survey-extended-deck-2018.pdf.

Department of Transportation (2018) *Fiscal Year 2018 Highlights* https://www.transportation.gov/sites/dot.gov/files/docs/mission/budget/281076/fiscal-year-2018-budget-highlights-book_0.pdf.

Dixon, P. (2010) *The One-Way Mirror Society: Privacy Implications of the New Digital Signage Networks.* World Privacy Forum http://www.worldprivacyforum.org/pdf/onewaymirrorsocietyfs.pdf.

Doherty, S. (2019, March 13) "The Activists Going on 'Birth Strike' to Protest Climate Change," *Vice* https://www.vice.com/en_ca/article/wjmkmz/the-activists-going-on-birth-strike-to-protest-climate-change.

References

The Dragonfly Initiative and Fairphone (2017) *Smartphone Material Profiles: Opportunities for Improvement in Ten Supply Chains* https://www.fairphone.com/wp-content/uploads/2017/05/Smart phoneMaterialProfiles_May2017.pdf.

Drouin, M., Kaiser, D. H, and Miller, D. A. (2012) "Phantom Vibrations Among Undergraduates: Prevalence and Associated Psychological Characteristics," *Computers in Human Behavior*, 28, no. 4: 1490–6.

Eco, U. (2014) "Foreword: Truth and the Mobile Phone," *Where Are You? An Ontology of the Cell Phone*. Ferraris, M. Trans. De Sanctis, S. New York: Fordham University Press, pp. vi–ix.

Edgeworth, M. (2010) "Beyond Human Proportions: Archaeology of the Mega and the Nano," *Archaeologies: Journal of the World Archaeological Congress*, 6, no. 1: 138–49.

El Gemayel, S. (2017) *Generation Zapped* https://www.youtube.com/watch?v=lUx9vqoJ95Y.

Environmental Health Trust (2018a) "Governments, Health Authorities and Schools Enacting Policy to Reduce Radiofrequency Radiation Exposures," *International Policy Briefing* https://ehtrust.org/wp-content/uploads/International-Policy-Precautionary-Act ions-on-Wireless-Radiation.pdf.

Environmental Health Trust (2018b) "Phonegate: French Government Data Indicates Cell Phones Expose Consumers to Radiation Levels Higher Than Manufacturers Claim" https://ehtrust.org/cell-phone-radiation-scandal-french-government-data-indicates-cell-phones-exposeconsumers-radiation-levels-higher-manufacturers-claim/.

Environmental Health Trust (n.d.) "Peer Reviewed Scientific Research on Wireless Radiation" https://ehtrust.org/science/research-on-wireless-health-effects/.

Environmental Health Trust (n.d.) "5G and the IOT: Scientific Overview of Human Health Risks" https://ehtrust.org/key-issues/

cell-phoneswireless/5g-networks-iot-scientific-overview-human-health-risks/.

Falcioni L., Bua, L., Tibaldi, E., Lauriola, M., De Angelis, L., Gnudi, F., Mandrioli, D., Manservigi, M., Manservisi, F., Manzoli, I., Menghetti, I., Montella, R., Panzacchi, S., Sgargi, D., Strollo, V., Vornoli, A., and Belpoggi, F. (2018) "Report of Final Results Regarding Brain and Heart Tumors in Sprague-Dawley Rats Exposed from Prenatal Life Until Natural Death to Mobile Phone Radiofrequency Field Representative of a 1.8 GHz GSM Base Station Environmental Emission," *Environmental Research*, 165: 496–503.

Farrell, J. (2019) "The Growth of Climate Change Misinformation in US Philanthropy: Evidence from Natural Language Processing," *Environmental Research Letters*, 14, no. 3: 1–10.

Federal Communications Commission (2018) *Wireless Devices and Health Concerns* https://www.fcc.gov/consumers/guides/wireless-devices-and-health-concerns.

Federal Communications Commission (n.d.) *Radio Frequency Safety* https://www.fcc.gov/general/radio-frequency-safety-0.

Feltman, R. (2016, May 27) "Do Cellphones Cause Cancer? Don't Believe the Hype," *The Washington Post* https://www.washingtonpost.com/news/speaking-of-science/wp/2016/05/27/do-cellphones-cause-cancer-dont-believe-the-hype/.

Fisher, D. J. (1988) *Romain Rolland and the Politics of Intellectual Engagement*. Berkeley: University of California Press.

Fisher, D. R. (2019) "#Fridays for Future," *Nature Climate Change* 9: 430–1.

Fogg, B. J. (2003) *Persuasive Technology: Using Computers to Change What We Think and Do*. Cambridge, Mass.: Springer.

Frampton, B. (2015, September 14) "Clickbait – The Changing Face of Online Journalism," *BBC News* https://www.bbc.com/news/uk-wales-34213693.

Funk, C. and Rainie, L. (2015) *Public and Scientists' Views on Science and Society*, Pew Research Center http://www.pewresearch.org/science/2015/01/29/public-and-scientists-views-on-science-and-society/.

Gagliano, M. (2013) "Green Symphonies: A Call for Studies on Acoustic Communication in Plants," *Behavioral Ecology*, 24, no. 4: 789–96.

Gallagher, M. (2019) "Childhood and the Geology of Media," *Discourse: Studies in the Cultural Politics of Education* https://doi.org/10.1080/01596306.2019.1620481.

Gault, M. (2018, April 23) "Europe Is Smuggling its E-Waste to Nigeria Inside Used Cars," *Motherboard* https://motherboard.vice.com/en_us/article/59jew8/e-waste-smuggling-nigeria.

Gibbs, S. (2018, January 8) "Apple Investors Call for Action Over iPhone 'Addiction' Among Children," *Guardian* https://www.theguardian.com/technology/2018/jan/08/apple-investors-iphone-addiction-children.

Gingerich, A. C. and Lineweaver, T. T. (2014) "OMG! Texting in Class = U Fail: (Empirical Evidence that Text Messaging During Class Disrupts Comprehension," *Teaching of Psychology*, 41, no. 1: 44–51.

Gladwell, V. F., Brown, D. K., Wood, C., Sandercock, G. R., and Barton, J. L. (2013) "The Great Outdoors: How a Green Exercise Environment Can Benefit All," *Extreme Physiology and Medicine*, 2: 3.

Glenza, J. (2019, January 23) "Revealed: The Free-Market Groups Helping the Tobacco Industry," *Guardian* https://www.theguardian.com/business/ng-interactive/2019/jan/23/free-market-think-tanks-tobacco-industry.

Gong, Y. (2019) *Manufacturing Towns in China*. Singapore: Palgrave Macmillan.

Good, J. E. (2016) "Creating iPhone Dreams: Annihilating E-waste Nightmares," *Canadian Journal of Communication*, 41, no. 4: 589–610.

References

Goranova, M. and Ryan, L. V. (2014) "Shareholder Activism: A Multidisciplinary Review," *Journal of Management*, 40, no. 5: 1230–68.

Governors Highway Safety Association (2018) *Distracted Driving Laws by State* https://www.ghsa.org/state-laws/issues/distracted%20 driving.

Grady, D. (2018, February 2) "Cancer Risk from Cellphone Radiation Is Small, Studies Show," *The New York Times*: A9.

Greenberg, P. (2018, October 31) "In Search of Lost Screen Time," *The New York Times* https://www.nytimes.com/2018/12/31/opin ion/smartphones-screen-time.html.

Greenpeace International (2012) *How Clean is Your Cloud?* https://www.greenpeace.org/international/publication/6986/how-clean-is-your-cloud/.

Grimes, D. R. (2018, July 21) "Mobile Phones and Cancer – The Full Picture," *Guardian* https://www.theguardian.com/technol ogy/2018/jul/21/mobile-phones-are-not-a-health-hazard.

Grossman, E. (2016) "The Body Burden: Toxics, Stresses and Biophysical Health," in Maxwell, R. (ed.) *The Routledge Companion to Labor and Media*. New York: Routledge, pp. 65–77.

Gupta, V. (2018, November 22) "Berkeley Decides to Keep Fighting for its Cellphone Right to Know Ordinance," *Medium* https://medium.com/@vishakha.vg.gupta/berkeley-decides-to-keep-fighting-for-its-cellphone-right-to-know-ordinance-66a3b 9dcd41e.

Hall, S. (2015, October 26) "Exxon Knew About Climate Change Almost 40 Years Ago," *Scientific American* https://www.scientific american.com/article/exxon-knew-about-climate-change-almost-40-years-ago/.

Hancock, S. (2009, October 10) "Iceland New Home of Server Farms?," *BBC News* http://news.bbc.co.uk/go/pr/fr/-/2/hi/progr ammes/click_online/8297237.stm.

References

Harkinson, J. (2016, May 27) "'Game-Changing' Study Links Cellphone Radiation to Cancer," *Mother Jones* https://www.mother jones.com/environment/2016/05/federal-study-links-cell-phone-ra diation-cancer/.

Harris, A. (2014) *Dragging Out the Best Deal: How Billion Dollar Margins Are Played Out on the Backs of Electronics Workers*, GoodElectronics https://goodelectronics.org/dragging-out-the-best-deal/.

Harris, J. (2018, December 10) "From Freecycling to Fairphones: 24 Ways to Lead an Anti-Capitalist Life in a Capitalist World," *Guardian* https://www.theguardian.com/environment/2018/dec/10/from-freecycling-to-fairphones-24-ways-to-lead-an-anti-capital ist-life-in-a-capitalist-world.

Hart, P. S. and Feldman, L. (2014) "Threat Without Efficacy? Climate Change on US Network News," *Science Communication,* 36, no. 3: 325–51.

Hartanto, A. and Yang, H. (2016) "Is the Smartphone a Smart Choice? The Effect of Smartphone Separation on Executive Functions," *Computers in Human Behavior*, 64: 329–36.

Haucke, F. V. (2018) "Smartphone-Enabled Social Change: Evidence From the Fairphone Case?," *Journal of Cleaner Production*, 197, Part 2: 1719–730.

Hauskeller, M. (2007) "The Reification of Life," *Genomics, Society and Policy*, 3, no. 2: 70–81.

Hembrooke, H. and Gay G. (2003) "The Laptop and the Lecture: The Effects of Multitasking in Learning Environments," *Journal of Computing in Higher Education*, 15, no. 1: 46–64.

Hertsgaard, M. and Dowie, M. (2018a, July 14) "The Inconvenient Truth About Cancer and Mobile Phones," *Guardian* https://www.theguardian.com/technology/2018/jul/14/mobile-phones-cancer-inconvenient-truths.

Hertsgaard, M. and Dowie, M. (2018b, March 29) "How Big Wireless

References

Made Us Think That Cell Phones Are Safe: A Special Investigation," *The Nation* https://www.thenation.com/article/how-big-wireless-made-us-think-that-cell-phones-are-safe-a-special-investigation/.

Hicklin, A. (2019, May 12) "Dr Ruth: 'Nobody Has Any Business Being Naked in Bed if They Haven't Decided to Have Sex'," *Guardian* https://www.theguardian.com/global/2019/may/12/still-talking-about-sex-dr-ruth-westheimer-interview.

Höjer, M., Eriksson, E., and Preist, C. (2018) "Special Issue on Information and Communications Technologies (ICT) for Sustainability," *Sustainability*, 10, no. 12 https://www.mdpi.com/journal/sustainability/special_issues/ICT.

Horton, C. (2019, April 17) "The Man Who Made Your iPhone Wants to Run Taiwan. A Sea Goddess Backs Him, He Says," *The New York Times* https://www.nytimes.com/2019/04/17/world/asia/terry-gou-foxcon-taiwan-presidential-race.html.

Howard, J. (2017, September 11) "When Kids Get Their First Cell Phones Around the World," *CNN* https://www.cnn.com/2017/12/11/health/cell-phones-for-kids-parenting-without-borders-explainer-intl/index.html.

Hussain, S. M., Wahid, A., Shah, M. A., Akhunzada, A., Khan, F., ul Amin, N., Arshad, S., and Ali, I. (2019) "Seven Pillars to Achieve Energy Efficiency in High-Performance Computing Data Centers," in Jan, M., Khan, F., and Alam, M., (eds.) *Recent Trends and Advances in Wireless and IoT-Enabled Networks*. Cham: Springer, pp. 93–105.

Hutton, J. (2011, September 30) "Mobile Phones Dominate in South Africa," *Nielsen Wire* http://blog.nielsen.com/nielsenwire/global/mobile-phones-dominate-in-south-africa.

International Agency for Research on Cancer (2011, May 31) "IARC Classifies Radiofrequency Electromagnetic Fields as Possibly Carcinogenic to Humans," Press Release 208 http://www.iarc.fr/en/media-centre/pr/2011/pdfs/pr208_E.pdf.

References

International Commission for Electromagnetic Safety (2012) *ICEMS Position Paper on the Cerebral Tumor Court Case* http://icems.eu/docs/ICEMS_Position_paper.pdf?f=/c/a/2009/12/15/MNHJ1B49KH.DTL.

International Energy Agency (2009) *Gadgets and Gigawatts: Policies for Energy Efficient Electronics – Executive Summary.* Paris: Organization for Economic Cooperation and Development.

International Energy Agency (2014) *More Data, Less Energy: Making Network Standby More Efficient in Billions of Connected Devices* http://www.iea.org/publications/freepublications/publication/MoreData_LessEnergy.pdf.

International Energy Agency (2017) *Digitalization and Energy* https://www.iea.org/digital/.

International Telecommunications Union (2018a) *Measuring the Information Society Report, Volume 1* https://www.itu.int/en/ITU-D/Statistics/Documents/publications/misr2018/MISR-2018-Vol-1-E.pdf.

International Telecommunications Union (2018b) *Setting the Scene for 5G: Opportunities and Challenges* https://www.itu.int/dms_pub/itu-d/opb/pref/D-PREF-BB.5G_01-2018-PDF-E.pdf.

INTERPHONE Study Group (2010) "Brain Tumor Risk in Relation to Mobile Telephone Use: Results of the INTERPHONE International Case-Control Study," *International Journal of Epidemiology*, 39, no. 3: 675–94.

Isaacson, W. (2011) *Steve Jobs*. New York: Simon & Schuster.

Jardim, E. (2017) *From Smartphones to Senseless: The Global Impact of 10 Years of Smartphones*, Greenpeace https://www.greenpeace.org/usa/wp-content/uploads/2017/03/FINAL-10YearsSmartphones-Report-Design-230217-Digital.pdf.

Jensen, R. (2007) "The Digital Provide: Information Technology, Market Performance, and Welfare in the South Indian Fisheries Sector," *Quarterly Journal of Economics*, 122, no. 3: 879–924.

References

Jiang, K., Ling, F., Feng, Z., Ma, C., Kumfer, W., Shao, C., and Wang, K. (2018) "Effects of Mobile Phone Distraction on Pedestrians' Crossing Behavior and Visual Attention Allocation at a Signalized Intersection: An Outdoor Experimental Study," *Accident Analysis and Prevention*, 115: 170–7.

Jindra, B., Hatani, F., Steger, T., and Hiemer, J. (2019) "Social Upgrading and Cooperative Corporate Social Responsibility in Global Value Chains: The Case of Fairphone in China," *Global Networks: A Journal of Transnational Affairs,* 19, no. 3: 371–93.

Kane, R. (2001) *Cellular Telephone Russian Roulette: A Historical and Scientific Perspective.* New York: Vantage Press.

Kara, S. (2018, October 12) "Is Your Phone Tainted by the Misery of 35,000 Children in Congo's Mines?," *Guardian* https://www.theguardian.com/global-development/2018/oct/12/phone-misery-children-congo-cobalt-mines-drc.

Khaki-Khatibi, F., Nourazarian, A., Ahmadi, F., Farhoudi, M., Savadi-Oskouei, D., Pourostadi, M., and Asgharzadeh, M. (2019) "Relationship Between the Use of Electronic Devices and Susceptibility to Multiple Sclerosis," *Cognitive Neurodynamics*, 13, no. 3: 287–92.

Kim, M.-H., Kim, H., and Paek, D. (2014) "The Health Impacts of Semiconductor Production: An Epidemiologic Review," *International Journal of Occupational and Environmental Health*, 20, no. 2: 95–114.

Kivrak, E. G., Yurt, K. K, Kaplan, A. A., Alkan, I., and Altun, G. (2017) "Effects of Electromagnetic Fields Exposure on the Antioxidant Defense System," *Journal of Microscopy and Ultrastructure*, 5, no. 4: 167–76.

Knutson, R. (2016, May 28) "US Cellphone Study Fans Cancer Worries," *Wall St Journal* https://www.wsj.com/articles/u-s-cell phone-study-fans-cancer-worries-1464393051.

References

Krugman, P. (2014, April 13) "Three Expensive Milliseconds," *The New York Times*: A23.

Kwon, M., Lee, J.-Y., Won, W.-Y., Park, J.-W., Min, J.-A., Hahn, C., Gu, X., Choi, J.-H., and Kim D.-J. (2013) "Development and Validation of a Smartphone Addiction Scale (SAS)," *PLoS ONE*, 8, no. 2: e56936.

Laber-Warren, E. (2018, December 24) "New Office Hours Aim for Well Rested, More Productive Workers," *The New York Times* https://www.nytimes.com/2018/12/24/well/mind/work-schedule-hours-sleep-productivity-chronotype-night-owls.html.

Laffen, B. and Kolata, G. (2016, May 27) "Will Your Cellphone Give You Cancer?," *The New York Times* https://www.nytimes.com/video/science/100000004441354/will-your-cellphone-give-you-cancer.html.

Lakoff, G. (2010) "Why it Matters How We Frame the Environment," *Environmental Communication*, 4, no. 1: 70–81.

La Monica, P. R. (2018, August 2) "Apple Reaches $1,000,000,000,000 Value," *CNN Business* https://money.cnn.com/2018/08/02/investing/apple-one-trillion-market-value/index.html.

Lapierre, M. A. and Lewis, M. N. (2018) "Should it Stay or Should it Go Now? Smartphones and Relational Health," *Psychology of Popular Media Culture*, 7, no. 3: 384–98.

Larmer, B. (2018, July 5) "E-Waste Offers an Economic Opportunity as Well as Toxicity," *The New York Times* https://www.nytimes.com/2018/07/05/magazine/e-waste-offers-an-economic-opportunity-as-well-as-toxicity.html.

Laudati, A. and Mertens, C. (2019) "Resources and Rape: Congo's (Toxic) Discursive Complex," *African Studies Review* https://doi.org/10.1017/asr.2018.126.

Lawrence, J. (2019, June 17). "The Life Expectancy of Major Household Appliances," *The Spruce* https://www.thespruce.com/lifespan-of-household-appliances-4158782.

References

Lawson, D. and B. B. Henderson. (2015) "The Costs of Texting in the Classroom," *College Teaching*, 63, no. 3: 119–24.

Lepawsky, J. (2015) "The Changing Geography of Global Trade in Electronic Discards: Time to Rethink the E-Waste Problem," *The Geographical Journal*, 181, no. 2: 147–59.

Lewandowsky S., Oreskes, N., Risbey, J. S., and Newell, B. R. (2015) "Seepage: Climate Change Denial and Its Effect on The Scientific Community," *Global Environmental Change*, 33: 1–13.

Lewis, M. (2014) *Flash Boys*. New York: W. W. Norton & Company.

Li, Y., Li, S., Zhou, Y., Meng, X., Zhang, J.-J., Xu, D.-P., and Li, H.-B. (2017) "Melatonin for the Prevention and Treatment of Cancer," *Oncotarget*, 8, no. 24: 39896–921.

Lin, Y.-H., Lin S.-H., Yang, C. C. H., and Kuo, T. B. J. (2017) "Psychopathology of Everyday Life in the 21st Century: Smartphone Addiction," in Montag, M. and Reuter, M. (eds.) *Internet Addiction: Neuroscientific Approaches and Therapeutic Implications Including Smartphone Addiction*. Cham: Springer, pp. 339–58.

Lu, D. (2019) "Everyday Modernity in China: From Danwei to the 'World Factory'," *Fudan Journal of the Humanities and Social Sciences*, 12, no. 1: 79–91.

Luntz, F. (2000) "The Environment: A Cleaner, Safer, Healthier America," The Luntz Research Companies https://www.mother jones.com/files/LuntzResearch_environment.pdf.

Lynch, M. J., Long, M. A., Barrett, K. L., and Stretesky, P. B. (2013) "Is it a Crime to Produce Ecological Disorganization? Why Green Criminology and Political Economy Matter in the Analysis of Global Ecological Harms," *British Journal of Criminology*, 53, no. 6: 997–1016.

Ma, H.-P., Chen, P.-L., Linkov, V. and Pai, C.-W. (2019) "Training or Battling a Monster of a Location-Based Augmented-Reality Game While Descending Stairs: An Observational Study of Inattentional

References

Blindness and Deafness and Risk-Taking Inclinations," *Frontiers in Psychology*, 10 https://doi.org10.3389/fpsyg.2019.00623.

Mahapatra, B., Saggurti, N., Halli, S. S., and Jain, A. K. (2012) "HIV Risk Behaviors Among Female Sex Workers Using Cell Phone for Client Solicitation in India," *Journal of AIDS and Clinical Research*, S1: 14.

Makower, J. (2014, March 3) "How GE and Apple Shareholders Became Tools for Climate Deniers," *GreenBiz* https://www.greenbiz.com/blog/2014/03/03/how-ge-and-apple-shareholders-became-tools-climate-deniers.

Malmodin, J. and Lundén, D. (2018) "The Energy and Carbon Footprint of the Global ICT and E&M Sectors 2010–2015," *Sustainability*, 10, no. 9: 3027.

Mann, M. and Toles, T. (2016) *The Madhouse Effect: How Climate Change Denial Is Threatening Our Planet, Destroying Our Politics, and Driving Us Crazy*. New York: Columbia University Press.

Marlon, J., Howe, P., Mildenberger, M., Leiserowitz, A., and Wang, X. (2018) "Estimated % of Adults Who Think Global Warming is Happening, 2018," *Yale Climate Opinion Maps 2018* http://climatecommunication.yale.edu/visualizations-data/ycom-us-2018/?est=happening&type=value&geo=county.

Marsh, S. (2018, June 22) "NHS to Launch the First Internet Addiction Clinic," *Guardian* https://www.theguardian.com/society/2018/jun/22/nhs-internet-addiction-clinic-london-gaming-mental-health.

Massey, K. A. (1979) "The Challenge of Nonionizing Radiation: A Proposal for Legislation," *Duke Law Journal*, 1: 105–89.

Maxwell, R. and Miller, T. (2012) *Greening the Media*. New York: Oxford University Press.

Maxwell, R. and Miller, T. (2016) "The Propaganda Machine Behind the Controversy Over Climate Science: Can You Spot the Lie in This Title?," *American Behavioral Scientist*, 60, no. 3: 288–304.

References

Mazzucato, M. (2015) *The Entrepreneurial State: Debunking Public vs. Private Sector Myths*. New York: Public Affairs.

McInerny, T. K. (2013, August 29) "Letter to Acting Chairwoman Clyburn (FCC) and Commissioner Hamburg (FDA)" http://apps.fcc.gov/ecfs/document/view?id=7520941318.

McSpadden, K. (2019, March 12) "'I Feel Naked Without My Phone' Should Be a Good Thing," *e27* https://e27.co/i-feel-naked-without-my-phone-should-be-a-good-thing-20190312/.

Mehta, A. (2018, May 16) "Here's How Much the US Has Spent Fighting Terrorism Since 9/11," *Defense News* https://www.defensenews.com/pentagon/2018/05/16/heres-how-much-the-us-has-spent-fighting-terrorism-since-911/.

Melnick, R. L. (2019) "Commentary on the Utility of the National Toxicology Program Study on Cell Phone Radiofrequency Radiation Data for Assessing Human Health Risks Despite Unfounded Criticisms Aimed at Minimizing the Findings of Adverse Health Effects," *Environmental Research*, 168: 1–6.

Melville H. (1855) "The Paradise of Bachelors and the Tartarus of Maids," *Harper's New Monthly Magazine*, 10: 670–8.

Michaels, R. A. (2019) "Telecommunications, Electromagnetic Fields, and Human Health," *Environmental Claims Journal,* 31, no. 2: 93–132.

Miller, C. C. (2014, April 5) "Technology's Man Problem," *The New York Times*: BU1.

Miller, D. and Dinan, W. (2015) "Resisting Meaningful Action on Climate Change: Think Tanks, 'Merchants of Doubt' and the 'Corporate Capture' of Sustainable Development," in Hansen, A. and Cox, R. (eds.) *Handbook of Environment and Communication*. London: Routledge, pp. 84–99.

Miller, T. (2015, April 14) "The Greens Are Not a Real Party of the Left – Here's Why," *The Conversation* https://theconversation.com/the-greens-are-not-a-real-party-of-the-left-heres-why-38614.

Mills, M. P. (2013) *The Cloud Begins with Coal: Big Data, Big Networks, Big Infrastructure, and Big Power*, National Mining Association and American Coalition for Clean Coal Electricity http://www.techpundit.com/wp-content/uploads/2013/07/Cloud_Begins_With_Coal.pdf?c761ac.

Mission Research (2017) "Marketplace: 2017 Cell Phone Risk-Knowledge Study, Research Report" https://ehtrust.org/wp-content/uploads/Marketplace-2017-Cell-Phone-Risk-Knowledge-Study.pdf.

Morin, E. (1999) *Seven Complex Lessons in Education for the Future*. Trans. Poller, N. Paris: United Nations Educational, Scientific and Cultural Organization.

Morley, D. (2017) *Communications and Mobility: The Migrant, the Mobile Phone and the Container Box*. Oxford: Wiley-Blackwell.

Moskowitz, J. M. (2018) "Ramazzini Institute Cell Phone Radiation Study Replicates NTP Study," Electromagnetic Radiation Safety https://www.saferemr.com/2018/03/RI-study-on-cell-phone.html.

Mouawad, J. and Galbraith, K. (2009, September 20) "Plugged-In Age Feeds Hunger for Electricity," *The New York Times* http://www.nytimes.com/2009/09/20/business/energy-environment/20efficiency.html?pagewanted=all.

Mueller, M. (1998) "The Shareholder Proposal Rule: Cracker Barrel, Institutional Investors, and the 1998 Amendments," *Stetson Law Review*, 28: 452–515.

Murphy, R. and Beland, L.-P. (2015, May 12) "How Smart is it to Allow Students to Use Mobile Phones at School?," *The Conversation* https://theconversation.com/how-smart-is-it-to-allow-students-to-use-mobile-phones-at-school-40621.

Nader, R. (1965) *Unsafe at Any Speed: The Designed-In Dangers of the American Automobile*. New York: Grossman Publishers.

Naftulin, J. (2016, July 13) "Here's How Many Times We Touch Our Phones Every Day," *Business Insider* https://www.businessin

sider.com/dscout-research-people-touch-cell-phones-2617-times-a-day-2016-7.

National Cancer Institute (2018) *Cell Phones and Cancer Risk*, National Institutes of Health https://www.cancer.gov/about-cancer/causes-prevention/risk/radiation/cell-phones-fact-sheet.

National Center for Statistics and Analysis (2017) *Distracted Driving 2015*, (Traffic Safety Facts Research Note. Report No. DOT HS 812 381) National Highway Traffic Safety Administration https://crashstats.nhtsa.dot.gov/Api/Public/ViewPublication/812381.

National Center for Statistics and Analysis (2018) *Distracted Driving 2016*, (Traffic Safety Facts Research Note. Report No. DOT HS 812 517) National Highway Traffic Safety Administration https://crashstats.nhtsa.dot.gov/Api/Public/Publication/812517.

National Institute of Environmental Health Sciences (2018, April) *NTP Cell Phone Studies – Experts Recommend Elevated Conclusions*, *Environmental Factor* https://factor.niehs.nih.gov/2018/4/feature/feature-2-cell-phone/index.htm.

National Safety Council (2018) *NSC Statement on IIHS Report on Increased Pedestrian Deaths* https://www.nsc.org/in-the-newsroom/nsc-statement-on-iihs-report-on-increased-pedestrian-deaths.

National Toxicology Program (2018a) *Cell Phone Radio Frequency Radiation*, National Institutes of Health https://ntp.niehs.nih.gov/results/areas/cellphones/index.html.

National Toxicology Program (2018b) *Peer Review of the Draft NTP Technical Reports on Cell Phone Radiofrequency Radiation*, National Institutes of Health https://ntp.niehs.nih.gov/ntp/about_ntp/trpanel/2018/march/peerreview20180328_508.pdf.

National Toxicology Program (2018c, March 26–8) *Cell Phone RFR Peer Review Panel Meeting Videos*, National Institutes of Health https://ntp.niehs.nih.gov/about/org/sep/trpanel/meetings/docs/2018/march/videos/videos.html.

Nicas, J., Chen, B. X., and Manjoo, F. (2018, June 5) "At Conference,

References

Apple Tells Developers It Still Wants to Be Different," *The New York Times*: B3.

Noble, D. (1995) *Progress Without People: New Technology, Unemployment, and the Message of Resistance*. Toronto: Between the Lines.

Nye, D. E. (1994) *American Technological Sublime*. Cambridge, Mass.: MIT Press.

Nye, D. E. (2006) "Technology and the Production of Difference," *American Quarterly*, 58, no. 3: 597–618.

Odeyingbo, O., Nnorom, I., and Deubzer, O. (2017) *Person in The Port Project: Assessing Import of Used Electrical and Electronic Equipment into Nigeria*, United Nations University, Bonn http://collections.unu.edu/eserv/UNU:6349/PiP_Report.pdf.

Ogan, C. L., Bashir, M., Camaj, L., Luo, Y., Gaddie, B., Pennington, R., Rana, S., and Salih, M. (2009) "Development Communication: The State of Research in an Era of ICTs and Globalization," *Gazette*, 71, no. 8: 655–70.

Olin Wright, E. (2012) "Transforming Capitalism Through Real Utopias," *American Sociological Review*, 78, no. 1: 1–25.

Ophir, E., Nass, C., and Wagner, A. D. (2009) "Cognitive Control in Media Multitaskers," *Proceedings of the National Academy of Sciences of the United States of America*, 106, no. 37: 1583–7.

Oreskes, N. and Conway, E. M. (2010) *Merchants of Doubt*. New York: Bloomsbury Press.

Organization for Economic Co-Operation and Development (2010) *Greener and Smarter: ICTs, the Environment and Climate Change*. Paris: Organization for Economic Co-Operation and Development.

Osnos, E. (2011, January 4) "Americanitis vs. Chinitis," *The New Yorker* https://www.newyorker.com/news/evan-osnos/americanitis-vs-chinitis.

Panagopoulos, D. J. (2019) "Comparing DNA Damage Induced by Mobile Telephony and Other Types of Man-Made Electromagnetic

Fields," *Mutation Research/Reviews in Mutation Research*, 781: 53–62.

Parents for Safe Technology (n.d.) *Worldwide Precautionary Action* http://www.parentsforsafetechnology.org/worldwide-countries-taking-action.html.

Pearce, F. (2018, April 3) "Energy Hogs: Can World's Huge Data Centers Be Made More Efficient?," *Yale Environment 360* https://e360.yale.edu/features/energy-hogs-can-huge-data-centers-be-made-more-efficient.

Peeples, L. (2018, July 11) "Wireless Industry Using First Amendment in Battle Against Safety Warnings," *In Depth NH*, New Hampshire Center for Public Interest Journalism http://indepthnh.org/2018/07/11/wireless-industry-avoids-safety-warnings/.

Perrin, A. and Jiang, J. (2018) *About a Quarter of US Adults Say They Are 'Almost Constantly' Online*, Pew Research Center http://www.pewresearch.org/fact-tank/2018/03/14/about-a-quarter-of-americans-report-going-online-almost-constantly/.

Pew Research Center (2018) *Mobile Fact Sheet* http://www.pewinternet.org/fact-sheet/mobile/.

Plumer, B. (2016, May 27) "Seriously, Stop With the Irresponsible Reporting on Cellphones and Cancer," *Vox* https://www.vox.com/2016/5/27/11797924/cellphones-cancer-bad-reporting.

Pockett, S. (2019) "Conflicts of Interest and Misleading Statements in Official Reports About the Health Consequences of Radiofrequency Radiation and Some New Measurements of Exposure Levels," *Magnetochemistry*, 5, no. 2 https://doi.org/10.3390/magnetochemistry5020031.

Poushter, J., Bishop, C., and Chwe, H. (2018) *Smartphone Ownership on the Rise in Emerging Economies*, Pew Research Center http://www.pewglobal.org/2018/06/19/2-smartphone-ownership-on-the-rise-in-emerging-economies/.

Prideaux, J. (2015, July 11) "The Age of Unreason," *The Economist* https://www.economist.com/special-report/2015/07/11/the-age-of-unreason.

Project Censored (2018, October 2) *How Big Wireless Convinced Us Cell Phones and Wi-Fi are Safe* https://www.projectcensored.org/4-how-big-wireless-convinced-us-cell-phones-and-wi-fi-are-safe/.

Public Broadcasting Service (2016, May 10) "Where Does America's E-Waste End Up? GPS Tracker Tells All," *News Hour* https://www.pbs.org/newshour/science/america-e-waste-gps-tracker-tells-all-earthfix.

Pun, N., Tse, T., and Ng, T. (2019) "Challenging Digital Capitalism: SACOM's Campaigns Against Apple and Foxconn as Monopoly Capital," *Information, Communication and Society*, 22, no. 9: 1253–68.

Qiu, J. L. (2010, December 16) *Deconstructing Foxconn*. China Labor Watch http://www.chinalaborwatch.org/newscast/74.

Qiu, J. L. (2016) *Goodbye iSlave: A Manifesto for Digital Abolition*. Champaign: University of Illinois Press.

Radulovic, V. (2018) "Portrayals in Print: Media Depictions of the Informal Sector's Involvement in Managing E-Waste in India," *Sustainability*, 10, no. 4: 966–95.

Rams, D. (2015, August 10) "Agbogbloshie: Ghana's 'Trash World' May be an Eyesore – But It's No Dump," *Ecologist* http://www.theecologist.org/News/news_analysis/2959811/agbogbloshie_ghanas_trash_world_may_be_an_eyesore_but_its_no_dump.html.

Readfearn, G. (2015, March 5) "Doubt Over Climate Science is a Product With an Industry Behind it," *Guardian* https://www.theguardian.com/environment/planet-oz/2015/mar/05/doubt-over-climate-science-is-a-product-with-an-industry-behind-it.

Renwick, D. W. S., Redman, T., and Maguire, S. (2013) "Green Human Resource Management: A Review and Research Agenda," *International Journal of Management Reviews*, 15, no. 1: 1–14.

References

Ritchie, H. and Roser, M. (2018, February) "Causes of Death," *Our World in Data* https://ourworldindata.org/causes-of-death.

Romundstad, P., Andersen, A., and Haldorsen, T. (2001) "Cancer Incidence Among Workers in the Norwegian Silicon Carbide Industry," *American Journal of Epidemiology*, 153, no. 10: 978–86.

Royal Dutch Shell (2019, April) *Industry Associations Climate Review* https://www.shell.com/sustainability/transparency/public-advoc acy-and-political-activity/_jcr_content/par/textimage.stream/1554 466210642/0a46ab13e36e99f8762ebb021bd72decec2f47b2/final-industry-association-climate-review-april-2019.pdf.

Rushkoff, D. (2016) *Throwing Rocks at the Google Bus.* New York: Penguin/Portfolio.

Rushkoff, D. (2019) *Team Human.* New York: WW Norton & Company.

Russell, J. (2013) *Resonance: Beings of Frequency* https://www.youtube.com/watch?v=9mK93gHFWXs.

Rusov, V. D., Lukin, K. A., Zelentsova, T. N., Linnik, E. P., Beglaryan, M. E., Smolyar, V. P., Filippov, M., and Vachev, B. (2012) "Can Resonant Oscillations of the Earth Ionosphere Influence the Human Brain Biorhythm?," *arXiv* https://arxiv.org/abs/1208.4970.

Russell, K. (2014, February 28) "Tim Cook Erupts After Shareholder Asks Him to Focus Only on Profit," *Business Insider* https://www.businessinsider.com/tim-cook-versus-a-conservative-think-tank-2014-2.

Sample, I. (2018, November 2) "Melatonin: The Body's Natural Sleep-Promoting Hormone," *Guardian* https://www.theguardian.com/science/2018/nov/02/melatonin-the-bodys-natural-sleep-promoting-hormone.

Sana, F., Weston, T., and Cepeda, N. (2013) "Laptop Multitasking Hinders Classroom Learning for Both Users and Nearby Peers," *Computers and Education*, 62, no. 1: 24–31.

References

Scheele, F. with de Haan, E. and Kiezebrink, V. (2016) *Cobalt Blues: Environmental Pollution and Human Rights Violations in Katanga's Copper and Cobalt Mines* Good Electronics https://www.somo.nl/cobalt-blues/.

Schiller, D. (2007) *How to Think About Information*. Champaign: University of Illinois Press.

Schlanger, Z. (2018, March 30) "We Now Have the First Clear Evidence Cell Phone Radiation Can Cause Cancer in Rats," *Quartz* https://qz.com/1241867/cell-phone-radiation-can-cause-cancer-in-rats-according-to-the-final-results-of-a-us-government-study/.

Schmidt, C. (2018, March 29) "New Studies Link Cell Phone Radiation with Cancer," *Scientific American* https://www.scientificamerican.com/article/new-studies-link-cell-phone-radiation-with-cancer/.

Schwartz, J. (2019, January 23) "Global Warming Concerns Rise Among Americans in New Poll," *The New York Times*: A18.

Seifter, A., Robbins, D., and Kalhoefer, K. (2016, March 7) "How Broadcast Networks Covered Climate Change in 2015," *Media Matters for America* https://www.mediamatters.org/research/2016/03/07/study-how-broadcast-networks-covered-climate-ch/208881.

Settembre, J. (2018, October 13) "You Can Save Big Money by Going on a Digital Detox at These Hotels and Restaurants," *MarketWatch* https://www.marketwatch.com/story/you-can-save-big-money-by-going-on-a-digital-detox-at-these-hotels-and-restaurants-2018-10-13.

Shaw, N. (2019, January 5) "For Ghana E-Waste Recyclers, a Safer Option Amid Toxic Fumes," Associated Press https://phys.org/news/2019-01-ghana-e-waste-recyclers-safer-option.html.

Shehabi, A., Smith, S.J., Horner, N., Azevedo, I., Brown, R., Koomey, J., Masanet, E., Sartor, D., Herrlin, M., and Lintner, W. (2016) *United States Data Center Energy Usage Report*, Lawrence Berkeley

National Laboratory, Berkeley, California. LBNL-1005775 http://eta-publications.lbl.gov/sites/default/files/lbnl-1005775_v2.pdf.

Shuren, J. (2018, February 2) *Statement from Jeffrey Shuren, M. D., J. D., Director of the FDA's Center for Devices and Radiological Health on the Recent National Toxicology Program Draft Report on Radiofrequency Energy Exposure*, US Food and Drug Administration https://www.fda.gov/newsevents/newsroom/pressannouncements/ucm595144.htm.

Silicon Valley Toxics Coalition (n.d.) *Electronic Industry Overview*. San Jose: Silicon Valley Toxics Coalition.

Silver, L. and Johnson, C. (2018) *Internet Connectivity Seen as Having Positive Impact on Life in Sub-Saharan Africa* Pew Research Center: Global Attitudes and Trends http://www.pewglobal.org/2018/10/09/internet-connectivity-seen-as-having-positive-impact-on-life-in-sub-saharan-africa/#table.

Silver, L. Smith, A., Johnson, C., Taylor, K., Jiang, J., Anderson, M., and Rainie, L. (2019) *Mobile Connectivity in Emerging Economies*, Pew Research Center https://www.pewinternet.org/2019/03/07/mobile-connectivity-in-emerging-economies/.

Smith, A. (2010, October 14) *Americans and Their Gadgets*, Pew Research Center http://www.pewinternet.org/2010/10/14/americans-and-their-gadgets/.

Starr, M. (2018, September 1) "Birds Can See Earth's Magnetic Fields, And Now We Know How That's Possible," *Science Alert* https://www.sciencealert.com/birds-see-magnetic-fields-cryptochrome-cry4-photoreceptor-2018.

Statt, N. (2016, September 2) "Google Confirms the End of its Modular Project Ara Smartphone," *The Verge* https://www.theverge.com/2016/9/2/12775922/google-project-ara-modular-phone-suspended-confirm.

Stefi, A. L., Margaritis, L. H., Skouroliakou, A. S., and Vassilacopoulou,

D. (2019) "Mobile Phone Electromagnetic Radiation Affects Amyloid Precursor Protein and α-Synuclein Metabolism in SH-SY5Y Cells," *Pathophysiology* https://doi.org/10.1016/j.pathophys.2019.02.004.

Stott, R., Smith, R., Williams, R., and Godlee, F. (2019) "Schoolchildren's Activism is a Lesson for Health Professionals," *British Medical Journal*, 365: 1–2.

Sumpter, D. (2018) *Outnumbered: From Facebook and Google to Fake News and Filter-Bubbles – The Algorithms That Control Our Lives*. London: Bloomsbury Sigma.

Sung-Won, Y. (2019, January 18) "Samsung Asked to Pay for Leukemia Victims," *The Korea Times* http://m.koreatimes.co.kr/phone/news/view.jsp?req_newsidx=183426.

Sunstein, C. R. (2017) *#republic: Divided Democracy in the Age of Social Media*. Princeton: Princeton University Press.

Suzuki, D. T. and Dressel, H. (2002) *Good News for a Change: Hope for a Troubled Planet*. Toronto: Stoddart.

Taplin, J. (2017) *Move Fast and Break Things: How Facebook, Google, and Amazon Cornered Culture and Undermined Democracy*. New York: Little, Brown and Company.

TechRepublic (n.d.) *The Internet of Things* https://www.techrepublic.com/topic/internet-of-things/.

Thiébaud, E., Hilty, L. M., Schluep, M., Böni, H. W., and Faulstich, M. (2018) "Where Do Our Resources Go? Indium, Neodymium, and Gold Flows Connected to the Use of Electronic Equipment in Switzerland," *Sustainability*, 10, no. 8: 2658.

Tranter, B. (2017) "It's Only Natural: Conservatives and Climate Change in Australia," *Environmental Sociology*, 3, no. 3: 274–85.

Trub, L. and Barbot, B. (2016) "The Paradox of Phone Attachment: Development and Validation of the Young Adult Attachment to Phone Scale (YAPS)," *Computers in Human Behavior*, 64: 663–72.

United Nations University/StEP Initiative (2016) "Guiding Principles

References

to Develop E-waste Management Systems and Legislation," *Solving the E-Waste Problem (StEP) White Paper* http://collections.unu.edu/eserv/UNU:6119/step_systems_and_legislation_final.pdf.

United States Government Accountability Office (2018) *Conflict Minerals*, GAO-18–457 https://www.gao.gov/assets/700/692851.pdf.

US Global Change Research Program (2018) *Climate Change Impacts in the United States*. US National Climate Assessment https://nca2014.globalchange.gov/downloads.

Valdesolo, P. (2015, October 27) "Scientists Study Nomophobia – Fear of Being Without a Mobile Phone," *Scientific American* https://www.scientificamerican.com/article/scientists-study-nomophobia-mdash-fear-of-being-without-a-mobile-phone/.

van den Brink, S., Kleijn, R., Tukker, A., and Huisman, J. (2019) "Approaches to Responsible Sourcing in Mineral Supply Chains," *Resources, Conservation and Recycling*, 145: 389–98.

Wäger, P., Schluep, M., and Müller, E. (2010) *RoHS Substances in Mixed Plastics from Waste Electrical and Electronic Equipment*, Swiss Federal Laboratories for Materials Science and Technology http://www.weee-forum.org/sites/default/files/documents/2010_rohs_substances_in_weee_plastics.pdf.

Wall, S., Wang, Z.-M., Kendig, T., Dobraca, D., and Lipsett, M. (2019) "Real-World Cell Phone Radiofrequency Electromagnetic Field Exposures," *Environmental Research*, 171: 581–92.

Ward, A. F., Duke, K., Gneezy, A., and Bos, M. W. (2017) "Brain Drain: The Mere Presence of One's Own Smartphone Reduces Available Cognitive Capacity," *Journal of the Association of Consumer Research*, 2, no. 2: 140–54.

Watts, J. (2018, October 8) "We Have 12 Years to Limit Climate Change Catastrophe, Warns UN," *Guardian* https://www.theguardian.com/environment/2018/oct/08/global-warming-must-not-exceed-15c-warns-landmark-un-report.

Wearden, G. and Carrington, D. (2019, January 24) "Teenage Activist Takes School Strikes 4 Climate Action to Davos," *Guardian* https://www.theguardian.com/environment/2019/jan/24/school-strikes-over-climate-change-continue-to-snowball.

Wegner, D. M. and Ward, A. F. (2013, December 1) "The Internet Has Become the External Hard Drive for Our Memories," *Scientific American* https://www.scientificamerican.com/article/the-internet-has-become-the-external-hard-drive-for-our-memories/.

West, J. (2015, March/April) "Inside the Chinese Boot Camps Designed to Break Video Game Addiction," *Mother Jones* https://www.motherjones.com/media/2015/06/chinese-internet-addiction-center-photos/.

Wilson, M. (2018, March 27) "Smartphones Are Killing the Planet Faster Than Anyone Expected," *Fast Company* https://www.fastcompany.com/90165365/smartphones-are-wrecking-the-planet-faster-than-anyone-expected.

Woo, C., Chung, Y., Chun, D., Han, S., and Lee, D. (2014) "Impact of Green Innovation on Labor Productivity and its Determinants: An Analysis of the Korean Manufacturing Industry," *Business Strategy and the Environment*, 23, no. 8: 567–76.

World Health Organization (2018) *Global Status Report on Road Safety 2018*, WHO Licence CC BYNC-SA 3.0 IGO https://www.who.int/violence_injury_prevention/road_safety_status/2018/en/.

World Health Organization (n.d.) *Electromagnetic Fields (EMF)* https://www.who.int/peh-emf/about/WhatisEMF/en/.

Wu, B. (2015, March 4) "Brianna Wu on Why Gamergate Trolls Won't Win," *Boston Globe Magazine* https://www.bostonglobe.com/magazine/2015/03/04/brianna-why-gamergate-tr.

Wu, D. (2019, April 16) "Foxconn's Gou Runs for Taiwan President, Citing Message from Sea Goddess," *Bloomberg* https://www.bloomberg.com/news/articles/2019-04-17/foxconn-s-gou-says-sea-goddess-backs-his-run-for-taiwan-leader.

References

Wyde, M., Cesta, M., Blystone, C., Elmore, S., Foster, P., Hooth, M., Kissling, G., Malarkey, D., Sills, R., Stout, M., Walker, N., Witt, K., Wolfe, M., and Bucher, J. (2016) *Report of Partial Findings from the National Toxicology Program Carcinogenesis Studies of Cell Phone Radiofrequency Radiation in Hsd: Sprague Dawley® SD rats (Whole Body Exposure)* https://phpa.health.maryland.gov/OEHFP/ EH/Shared%20Documents/CEHPAC/December%2013%20 CEHPAC%20Comments%20Part%201.pdf.

Yildirim, C. and Correia, A.-P. (2015) "Exploring the Dimensions of Nomophobia: Development and Validation of a Self-Reported Questionnaire," *Computers in Human Behavior*, 49: 130–7.

Zook, M. and Grote, M. H. (2017) "The Microgeographies of Global Finance: High-Frequency Trading and the Construction of Information Inequality," *Environment and Planning A: Economy and Space*, 49, no. 1: 121–40.

Index

Index